Visual Science
Encyclopedia

Earthquakes
and
Volcanoes

▲ Popocatepetl in Mexico during
a period of relative inactivity.

How to use this book

Every word defined in this book can be found in alphabetical order on pages 3 to 47. There is also a full index on page 48. A number of other features will help you get the most out of the *Visual Science Encyclopedia*. They are shown below.

Here you will find the first word defined on any left-hand page.

Each word is shown in bold so it is easy to find.

Other words defined in the book are highlighted in bold.

Plus, many entries point to related words of interest.

Here you will find the last word defined on any right-hand page.

Each new letter of the alphabet is clearly marked to help you find the word you are looking for quicker.

Illustrations for some words complement the text and provide further information on a topic.

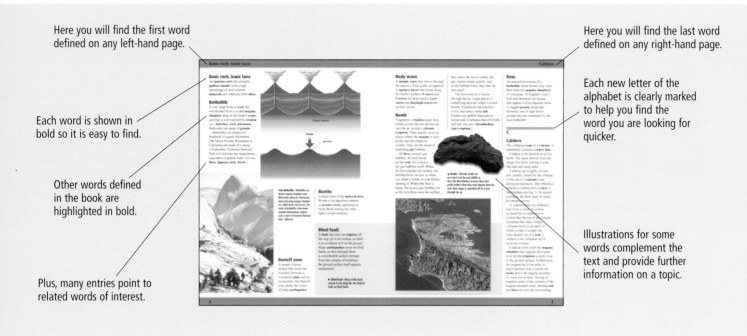

Acknowledgments

Grolier Educational
First published in the United States in 2002 by Grolier Educational, Sherman Turnpike, Danbury, CT 06816

Copyright © 2002
Atlantic Europe Publishing Company Ltd.

All rights reserved. No part of this publication may be reproduced, stored in a retrieval system, or transmitted in any form or by any means— electronic, mechanical, photocopying, recording, or otherwise—without prior permission of the publisher.

Author
Brian Knapp, BSc, PhD

Art Director
Duncan McCrae, BSc

Senior Designer
Adele Humphries, BA, PGCE

Editors
Lisa Magloff, BA, and Mary Sanders, BSc

Illustrations
David Woodroffe

Designed and produced by
EARTHSCAPE EDITIONS

Reproduced in Malaysia by
Global Color

Printed in Hong Kong by
Wing King Tong Company Ltd.

Library of Congress Cataloging-in-Publication Data
Visual Science Encyclopedia
   p. cm.
   Includes indexes.
   Contents: v. 1. Weather—v. 2. Elements—v. 3. Rocks, minerals, and soil— v. 4. Forces—v. 5. Light and sound— v. 6. Water—v. 7. Plants—v. 8. Electricity and magnetism—v. 9. Earth and space— v. 10. Computers and the Internet—v. 11. Earthquakes and volcanoes—v. 12. Heat and energy.
   ISBN 0-7172-5595-6 (set: alk. paper)—ISBN 0-7172-5596-4 (v. 1: alk. paper)—ISBN 0-7172-5597-2 (v. 2: alk. paper)—ISBN 0-7172-5598-0 (v. 3: alk. paper)—ISBN 0-7172-5599-9 (v. 4: alk. paper)—ISBN 0-7172-5600-6 (v. 5: alk. paper)—ISBN 0-7172-5601-4 (v. 6: alk. paper)—ISBN 0-7172-5602-2 (v. 7: alk. paper)—ISBN 0-7172-5603-0 (v. 8: alk. paper)—ISBN 0-7172-5604-9 (v. 9: alk. paper)—ISBN 0-7172-5605-7 (v. 10: alk. paper)—ISBN 0-7172-5606-5 (v. 11: alk. paper)—ISBN 0-7172-5607-3 (v. 12: alk. paper)
   1. Science—Encyclopedias, Juvenile.
[1. Science—Encyclopedias.] I. Grolier Educational (Firm)

QI21.V58 2001
503—dc21
                              2001023704

Picture credits
All photographs are from the Earthscape Editions photolibrary except the following:
(c=center t=top b=bottom l=left r=right)
USGS 3t, 10, 15tr, 27t, 28t, 47b (Griggs, J.D.), 4br, 44tr (Casadevall, T.J.), 15tl (Austin Post), 23b (Decker, R.), 26b, 28c, (Heliker, C.C.), 33tr (Mattox, T.N.), 4b, 7b, 12cr, 13tr, 17t, 18t, 22b, 33b, 36t, 42; *NASA* 36c, 39t; *NASA/USGS* 46.

This product is manufactured from sustainable managed forests. For every tree cut down, at least one more is planted.

A

Aa lava

A type of **lava** with a broken, bouldery surface. Aa lava forms from a type of **basalt** lava that is relatively sticky. It tends to form a crust on the surface of flowing lava, which is then broken up by the moving lava below. (*Compare with:* **Pahoehoe lava**.)

Acceleration

The rate of change of the ground movement during an **earthquake**. The ground movement speeds up from its rest position as a **seismic wave** passes through. The faster the ground speeds up, the more damage the earthquake is likely to do.

Acid lava/acid rock

A type of **lava** or **igneous rock** that is mainly made up of light-colored **minerals** and is more than two-thirds **silica** (for example, **rhyolite** and **granite**). (*See also:* **Viscous, viscosity**.)

Active fault

A **fault** that is known to have moved in historic times.
(*See also:* **Seismic gap**.)

Active volcano

(*See:* **Volcanic activity**.)

Aftershock

An **earthquake** that happens after the **main shock**. Major earthquakes are always followed by a number of aftershocks that decrease in number over the following days and weeks. In general, the larger the main shock, the larger and more numerous the aftershocks, and the longer they continue.

▶▼ **Aa lava—** Aa lava is thick and develops a crust that breaks up as the lava below moves.

Lava moves very slowly, and a thick crust forms on the surface.

Boulders of lava

Agglomerate

A **rock** made from the compacted particles thrown out by a **volcano** (for example, **tephra**).

Alkaline rock

A type of **igneous rock** containing less than half **silica** and normally dominated by dark-colored **minerals**. (*See also:* **Gabbro**.)

Amplification

The magnification of an **earthquake** when **seismic waves** travel through soft ground. Soft, wet materials such as bay and lake deposits amplify the waves greatly, causing the ground to wobble like jelly. Places such as Mexico City and the bayfront (Marina) area of San Francisco, California, are especially at risk from this effect.

Amplitude

A measurement of the strength of an **earthquake**. Amplitude is measured on a **seismograph**. Large peaks on the trace, or **seismogram**, indicate a large amplitude and a strong quake.

Amygdule

A bubble in a **volcanic rock** filled with secondary **minerals** such as calcite or **quartz**. (*See also:* **Vesicle**.)

Andesite

A type of **lava** whose properties are halfway between **rhyolite** and **basalt**. Andesite is the most common form of lava found in **explosive volcanoes**. Its name comes from its association with the active Andean volcanoes.

Andesite makes up the main material of a **composite volcanic cone**. Andesitic lava contains many cavities. It may be light colored, but is normally dark, especially brown. Although it is not a particularly **acid lava**, it is still reasonably sticky and so forms short **lava flows** that usually develop into **tongues** that move short distances down the sides of volcanic cones. (*See also:* **Diorite**.)

Arc

A crescent pattern of **volcanoes** that sometimes forms when an oceanic **plate** collides with a continental plate and then slides down underneath it. (*See also:* **Island arc** and **Subduction zone**.)

Ash

A fine, gray material (less than 2mm across) that is almost dustlike. It is thrown out of a **volcano** during an **explosive eruption**.

Ash is produced from sticky **lava** that is full of **gases**. As this sticky lava comes up the **vent** of the volcano, it is under great pressure. Then, as it reaches the surface, the pressure is released, and the gases in the lava expand almost instantly, tearing the sticky lava apart, and creating a fine spray that is shot high into the air.

The tiny bits of lava cool very quickly into solid **rock** to produce a variety of materials called **tephra**. The finest form of tephra is called ash.

When ash falls, it is still very powdery, but it slowly compacts over the years into new rock (*see:* **Tuff**).

The finest particles of ash are easily carried large distances by the wind.

Because ash comes from rising **magma**, the ash that is exploded out of a volcano and the lava that flows out are two forms of exactly the same material.

Good examples of ash clouds that have been formed in recent years include Mount Pinatubo in 1991 and Mount St. Helens in 1980 (*see:* **Volcanic activity**).

Mount Pinatubo produced fine ash that went straight up into the air. Much of it fell back around the volcano, blanketing the slopes and nearby landscape in light gray ash, but some of it stayed in the air for a long time. It is thought that it helped block out the Sun's rays. In the following year the average world temperature fell by 0.5°C. After this the ash was washed out of the air, and the world's temperatures went up again.

◀▼ **Ash**—Ash makes up much of the visible material ejected during an explosive eruption, such as that of Mount Pinatubo, shown below. It is fine enough to be carried some distance from an eruption. During an eruption it may settle out on roads and block them. If thick ash settles on roofs, the weight may cause the building to collapse.

▶ **Basalt**—Basalt is the most common volcanic rock. Most basalt is erupted on the ocean floors. However, much basalt is also found in places where this runny lava once flooded over the land. Here it forms thick layers of rock that, when exposed, show distinctive columns. Hells Canyon, Idaho, is one place that has these columns.

Ash flow

A dense, hot avalanche of **rock** fragments, **gas**, and **ash** that travel rapidly down the sides of a **volcano** (it is the same as **pyroclastic flow**).

Asthenosphere

The weak part of the upper **mantle** below the **lithosphere**. It is the place in which it is thought that molten materials move slowly. It is the source of much of the world's magma and the "engine" for the movement of the world's tectonic **plates**.

Augite

A dark-green **silicate mineral** containing calcium, sodium, iron, aluminum, and magnesium. Commonly found in dark-colored **igneous rocks** such as **gabbro**. (*See also:* **Ferromagnesian minerals**.)

B

Basalt

A black, **basic**, fine-grained, **igneous volcanic rock**. Basaltic **lava** often contains **vesicles**. (*See also:* **Aa lava** and **Pahoehoe lava**.)

Basalt is the most common rock on the Earth's surface, covering all of the world's ocean floors. It is produced at the boundaries of the world's great tectonic **plates** and pours out onto the seabed as the plates pull apart. Hawaii and Iceland are volcanic islands that are made entirely from basalt. Basalt cools to form very distinctive hexagonal columns. Although basalt columns are found mainly close to the **fissures** of ocean floors, they are also found on land. Iceland and Hawaii are two places that frequently experience **eruptions** of basalt.

Historically, basalt has been ejected from the **mantle** to form enormous floods of lava called **flood basalts**, which have consolidated into vast black sheets (*see:* **Supervolcano**). Flood basalts are also called basalt plateaus or traps. The name trap comes from the world's largest region of flood basalts, the Deccan Traps, India. Large areas of flood basalts also occur in the Columbia-Snake River region of the northwestern United States and in the Paraná Basin of South America.

Because basalt is a runny form of lava, the eruptions that it produces are not explosive or violent; and since they mainly occur on the ocean bed, many of them go unnoticed.

Basalts are black because they are made of **minerals** that contain iron known as **ferromagnesian minerals**. The crystals in basalt are usually too small to be seen without a magnifying glass or a hand lens. As a result basalt appears to be a uniformly black rock. Occasionally, basalt contains larger crystals that can be seen as small, shiny minerals. (*See also:* **Hornblende**.)

Basic rock, basic lava

An **igneous** rock (for example, **gabbro**, **basalt**) with a high percentage of dark-colored **minerals** and relatively little **silica**.

Batholith

A very large body of **rock** that was formed from a cooled **magma chamber** deep in the Earth's **crust**, and that is now exposed by **erosion** (*see:* **Intrusive rock, intrusion**). Batholiths are made of **granite**.

Batholiths can extend for hundreds of square kilometers. The Sierra Nevada Mountains in California are made of a string of batholiths. Yosemite National Park in California has magnificent exposures of granite rock. (*See also:* **Boss**; **Igneous rock**; **Stock**.)

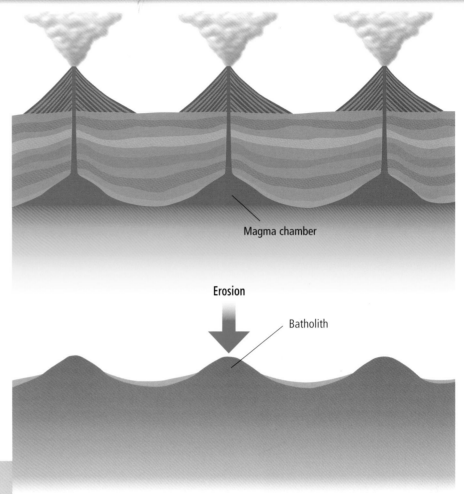

Magma chamber

Erosion

Batholith

◄▲ **Batholith**—Batholiths are former magma chambers now filled with cold rock. Protrusions above the main magma chamber are called stocks and bosses. The rocks of batholiths often make rounded mountainous regions, such as here in Yosemite National Park, California.

Biotite

A black form of the **mineral mica**. Biotite is an important mineral in **granite rocks**, appearing as black flecks among the other light-colored minerals.

Blind fault

A **fault** that does not **rupture** all the way up to the surface, so there is no evidence of it on the ground. Many **earthquakes** occur on blind faults, so that although there is considerable surface damage from the collapse of buildings, the ground surface itself appears undisturbed.

▶ **Blind fault**—Many of the faults (shown in red) along the San Andreas Fault are blind faults.

Benioff zone

A steeply sloping surface that marks the boundary between a continental **plate** and an ocean plate. The Benioff zone marks the source of many **earthquakes**.

Body wave

A **seismic wave** that moves through the interior of the Earth, as opposed to **surface waves** that travel along the Earth's surface. **P waves** and **S waves** are body waves, **Love waves** and **Rayleigh waves** are surface waves.

Bomb

Fragments of **tephra** larger than 64mm across that are thrown up into the air during a **volcanic eruption**. They usually occur in places where the **magma** is very sticky and the eruptions violent. They are the result of exploding **gas** bubbles.

All **lava** contains gas bubbles. As lava moves up the **vent** of a volcano, the gas bubbles swell. When the lava reaches the surface, the bubbles burst out just as when you shake a bottle of soda before opening it. Where the lava is runny, the excess gas bubbles out as the lava flows over the surface.

But where the lava is sticky, the gas cannot escape quietly; and as the bubbles burst, they tear the lava apart.

The lava cools as it travels through the air. Large pieces of solidifying lava are called volcanic bombs. Explosions that produce a very fine spray create **ash**. Cinders are pebble-sized pieces whose size is between that of bombs and ash. (*See also:* **Strombolian-type eruption**.)

▲ **Bomb**—Volcanic bombs do not travel very far and solidify as they fall. Nevertheless, because they were partly molten when they were thrown from the vent, their shape is smoothed off by travel through the air.

San Francisco

San Andreas Fault

Boss

An upward protrusion of a **batholith**. Some bosses may once have been the **magma chambers** of volcanoes. In England Land's End and Dartmoor are bosses that appear to form separate areas of rugged **granite** landscape. However, out of sight below ground they are connected by the main batholith.

C

Caldera

The collapsed **cone** of a **volcano**. It sometimes contains a **crater lake**.

Caldera is the Spanish word for kettle. The name derives from the shape of a kettle, having a wide, flat base and steep sides.

Calderas are roughly circular pits, usually caused by the collapse of the top of a **volcanic** cone during an explosion. The difference between a caldera and a **crater** is that calderas are big. To be named a caldera, the floor must be many kilometers across.

A caldera forms in a different way from a crater. A caldera is caused by an explosion so violent that the top of the volcano, including the crater, simply collapses back in on itself. So, while a crater is simply the cone-shaped top of a **vent**, a caldera is the collapsed top of an entire volcano.

Calderas form when the **magma chamber** that supplies the liquid rock for the **eruption** is quite close to the ground surface. Furthermore, the magma has to be under so much pressure that it causes the **rocks** above the magma chamber to crack and weaken. During an eruption some of the contents of the magma chamber erupt, sending **ash** and **lava** out over the surrounding

▼ **Caldera**—A caldera is a large sunken area at the top of a volcano. It is not just a large vent, but the collapsed top of the volcano. The diagrams illustrate the formation of Crater Lake, Oregon, shown in the photograph below.

1—The volcano erupts violently, so that the rocks are weakened. At the same time, the lava pours out of the vent so fast that the magma chamber is left partly empty.

2—The weight of the volcano's cone causes it to collapse in on the magma chamber, producing a vast pit that can, over the following centuries, fill with water.

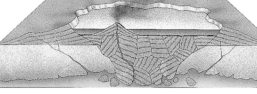

countryside. As a result, the magma chamber is partly empty. Normally, the magma chamber would be slowly filled from below. However, if the magma chamber is close to the ground surface, the volcano large and heavy, and the rocks above weak, then the weight of the volcano might be enough to cause the whole top of the cone to collapse down into the partly empty chamber before it can refill.

Many volcanoes remain active even after a catastrophic event like the collapse of their cones. In time a new cone will grow from the center of the caldera.

Well-developed calderas include the summit area of Vesuvius in Italy. One of the most famous calderas containing a lake is Crater Lake in Oregon. The rim of the crater is 11km across, 42km around, and is partly filled with a lake nearly 600m deep. The lake contains an island, Wizard Island, which is the tip

of the new cone that is growing from the lake floor to replace the cone that collapsed about 5,000 years ago. Although it looks small, the new cone is 826m high; the lower 600m are submerged in the lake. The lake and surrounding area make up Crater Lake National Park.

To the northeast lies Yellowstone National Park, with its famous **geysers**. These geysers have formed on the floor of another caldera. Geysers are common here because the rock was severely **fractured** during the formation of the caldera, allowing rain and snow to seep down to the hot rocks above the magma chamber.

Central vent volcano

A steep-sided **volcano**, usually formed into a **cone** and made of both **lava** and **ash**. It is fed by a single vertical pipe, or **vent**. Alternative terms are **composite volcano** and **stratovolcano**.

Cinder cone

A **volcanic cone** made entirely of volcanic cinders and **bombs**. Cinder cones have very steep sides.

If you walk on this kind of cone, it feels like walking over the cinders from a coke fire. The cinders contain many **gas** bubbles that makes them lightweight.

Cinder cones often form very quickly, although few are large. Many cinder **eruptions** build small cones on the sides of existing **volcanoes** (*see:* **Parasitic cone**). Very occasionally they make up entire volcanic mountains. The famous volcano Paricutin in Mexico grew 300m in one year (1944) and was 410m high when it stopped erupting eight years later. Because it is all made of the same rough material, the sides stand at the same slope—about 33°—more than twice as steep as most volcanoes.

One area with a large number of cinder cones is in Idaho, in a place called the Craters of the Moon.

▲ **Cinder cone**—Cinder cones are relatively small volcanic cones. This example is from the Craters of the Moon National Monument, Idaho.

Colliding boundary

One of the edges of the Earth's tectonic **plates** where two continental plates collide. Usually one plate is pushed under the other. The boundary is a common location for **earthquakes** and explosive **volcanoes**, **island arcs**, and **ocean trenches**. Colliding boundaries also coincide with **subduction zones**. The most active colliding boundary lies around the Pacific Ocean (*see:* **Pacific Ring of Fire**).

Complex volcano

A **volcano** that has two or more **vents**.

Composite volcano

A steep-sided **volcano**, usually formed into a **cone** and made of both **lava** and **ash** in alternating layers. (*See also:* **Central vent volcano** and **Stratovolcano**.)

Cone

The shape of an **explosive** type of **volcano**. A **caldera** is a collapsed cone. (*See also:* **Parasitic cone**.)

▼ **Cone**—This is Mt. Shasta, one of the most prominent cones in the Cascade Mountains.

◄ **Crater**—A crater lies in the uppermost part of the cone and is the top of the vent. Notice the lava at the bottom of this crater and the many layers of rock (the remains of former eruptions) showing in the sides. This provides evidence that a volcano builds up as a result of many eruptions.

Core

The central region of the Earth. It is about 6,000km in diameter and is surrounded by the **mantle**.

Crater

The funnel-shaped depression surrounding the top of the **vent** in a violently exploding type of **volcano**.

As the **magma** rushes out of the vent, it tends to rip away the top of the vent, widening it and forming a **cone**. The exact shape and size of the crater depend on the violence of the **eruption**. At the end of the eruption the crater will have very steep sides. The vent will be blocked by the remains of the **lava** from the eruption, giving the appearance of a crater floor.

Over time the **rock** in the walls of the crater is attacked by the forces of weather, and chunks of rock from the sides fall into the bottom of the crater.

New craters thus have steep sides and an irregular floor, while old craters have less steep sides and a flat floor.

Most craters on the top, or summit, of volcanoes are really very small compared to the size of the volcano, being just a few hundred meters across and a hundred meters or so deep.

Many volcanoes have craters. Kilauea is a mountain on Hawaii that erupts almost every year. The material that comes from the vent, in the form of a **lava fountain**, is runny **basalt**. There are never any explosions.

During an eruption a **lava lake** may build up in the crater. Sometimes a cone may form, made from the cooling rock of a lava fountain.

A much larger "crater" is created by the collapse of the top of the volcano during a violent eruption. It produces a **caldera**.

Crater lake

A lake found inside a **crater**, but more usually inside a **caldera**.

Creep

The slow movement of one part of the Earth's **crust** past another. It happens along a deep **fracture** called a **fault** line. Parts of the Earth's crust that are creeping past one another do not tend to have large **earthquakes**.

Crust

The outermost layer of the Earth. The Earth is made up of three main layers: The very thin crust of brittle **rocks** that cover the surface; the central molten **core**; and a thick layer in between called the **mantle**.

The mantle and core together make up nearly the entire distance to the center of the Earth. By contrast, the crust makes up less than 1% of the Earth's volume and has an average thickness of about 35km. The crust can be as little as 5km thick under the oceans, but more than 100km thick under continents.

The uppermost 15km to 35km of the continental crust is especially brittle and is the **focus** of most **shallow earthquakes**.

The crust is broken up into a number of huge slabs, each of which contains both continents and ocean floors (*see:* **Lithosphere**). These pieces are called **plates** or tectonic plates. The plates are moved around by the slow flow of the upper mantle (*see:* **Asthenosphere**). This process is called **plate tectonics**.

Volcanoes and **earthquakes** occur where plates collide. Volcanoes also occur where plates pull apart, and earthquakes can occur where plates slide past one another.

The **magma** that feeds volcanoes originally begins at the top of the mantle. However, most continental volcanoes are fed from **magma chambers** that are near the top of the crust.

(*See also:* **Feldspars** and **Mohorovicic discontinuity**.)

Crystal

A **mineral** that has a regular geometric shape and is bounded by smooth, flat faces. (*See also:* **Phenocryst**.)

D

Destructive plate boundary

A zone where **plates** collide, and one plate is forced down below another. (*See also:* **Benioff zone** and **Plate tectonics**.)

Dike

A wall-like sheet of **intrusive igneous rock** (typically **diorite**) that cuts across other **rocks**. A dike is formed entirely underground.

There are several causes for dike formation. One form of dike occurs at the end of a **fissure**

eruption. When the eruption stops, the **magma** in the **fissure** will cool and turn to rock. This wall of rock makes a dike.

Dikes may also occur in areas surrounding the **magma chamber** that are not connected with the main **vent**. They occur when the rock enclosing the magma chamber **fractures**, allowing magma to flow into the surrounding rock.

Most dikes are between 2m and 6m thick.

(*See also:* **Erosion** and **Sill**.)

Dike swarm

A collection of hundreds or thousands of parallel **dikes**.

The largest number of dikes in the world occur under the oceans and are the result of **fissure eruptions**. They make up most of the ocean **crust**.

Dikes also occur on land close to active **volcanoes**. Continental areas containing dike swarms include northwestern Scotland and Northern Ireland.

Diorite

An **igneous rock** that forms underground. It has properties in between **gabbro** and **granite**; it has the same composition as the **lava** called **andesite**. Diorite is the typical **rock** of **dikes** and **sills**. Diorite is a medium- to coarse-grained igneous rock that contains about two-thirds **feldspar** and one-third dark-colored **ferromagnesian minerals**.

Dormant volcano

A **volcano** that shows no signs of **volcanic activity** today but that has been active in the recent past. It is hard to give an exact status to any volcano because it may erupt only once in several hundred years. Geologists call a volcano dormant when it has not **erupted** in the past 100 or more years, but the **ash** and **lava** of its **cone** suggest (geologically) recent activity. A dormant volcano may become active again with little warning.

▼▶ **Dike**—A dike is a band of igneous rock that cuts across other rocks. This wall of rock is a dike.

Dike

E

Earthquake

The sudden movement of a **plate** along a **fault** and the ground shaking that is caused by it.

An earthquake is a tear in the rock, often called a **rupture**. Earthquakes can occur as deep as 750km below the surface. Most, however, are more shallow, being less than 70km deep.

There are 500,000 detectable earthquakes in the world each year. Of those, 100,000 can be felt, and about 100 cause damage. Ten percent of all the world's earthquakes occur in Japan.

The largest recorded earthquake in the United States was a **magnitude** 9.2 that struck Prince William Sound, Alaska, on March 28, 1964. The largest recorded earthquake in the world was a magnitude 9.5 in Chile on May 22, 1960. The earliest reported earthquake in California was felt in 1769 by the expedition of Gaspar de Portola while the group was camping near Los Angeles.

The world's most destructive earthquake in historic times occurred in central China in 1557. It happened in a region of soft rock. The houses and caves where people lived simply crumbled away during the earthquake, and some 830,000 people died. In 1976 another deadly earthquake struck in Tangshan, China, and more than 250,000 people were killed.

Most earthquakes occur where great slabs of the Earth's surface, called **plates**, move past one another. The majority of earthquakes occur where the Pacific Ocean plate pushes under the surrounding continents (part of which includes California). Earthquakes are often accompanied

◄▶ **Earthquake**—Sometimes a fault can be seen at the surface, but more often it is a blind fault that never reaches the surface, and cracks are movements of the soil rather than the actual fault.

▼ **Earthquake**—The focus of an earthquake is usually where two crustal plates are moving relative to one another. This diagram shows an earthquake on the Benioff Zone, the region separating a continental from an oceanic plate.

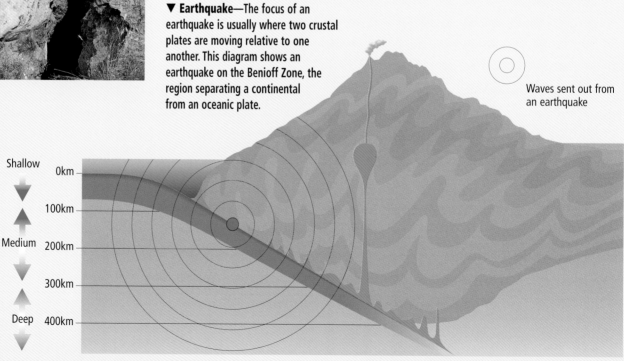

Waves sent out from an earthquake

Shallow
0km
100km
Medium 200km
300km
Deep 400km

by increased **volcanic activity**; and because this is also the most active **volcanic** region of the world, this zone is called the **Pacific Ring of Fire**.

A rupture sets off many kinds of vibrations, called **seismic waves**. Some travel through the Earth and are called **body waves**, while others travel near the surface and are called **surface waves**. Body waves are used to pinpoint the starting point (also called the **hypocenter** or **focus**) of the earthquake, while surface waves are the ones that cause damage due to ground shaking. (*See also:* **Acceleration**; **Amplification**; **Epicenter**; **Shock wave**.)

Earthquakes are measured and located using instruments called **seismographs**. For this, readings from three stations are needed. The waves are analyzed to see how long it took between the first waves (**P waves**) and the second waves (**S waves**) to arrive. From this data the distance to the earthquake focus can be calculated. Multiplying the time in seconds between the arrival of the two waves by eight gives the distance in kilometers. Three such measurements locate the focus accurately by a method called triangulation.

Earthquakes and their effects are measured using two scales. The amount of energy in the earthquake is measured on the **Richter scale**, while the damage that the earthquake does is measured on the **Modified Mercalli scale**.

(*For more on the effects of earthquakes see*: **Ground failure**; **Liquefaction**; **Seiche**; **Seismic deformation**; **Tsunami**.)

(*See also:* **Aftershock**; **Mainshock**; **Seismic gap**; **Seismic zone**; **Shadow zone**; **Shallow earthquake**.)

▶ **Earthquake**—Ground movement can have very severe effects on buildings. This one has tilted as a result of ground liquefaction.

Ejecta

A general term for anything thrown into the air from a **volcano** during an **eruption**. Ejecta is also another word for **tephra**.

Epicenter

The point on the Earth's surface directly above the **focus** (**hypocenter**) of an **earthquake**.

▼ **Epicenter**—The epicenter is the point on the surface directly above the focus of the earthquake.

Erosion

The twin processes of breaking down a **rock** (called weathering) and then removing the debris (called transporting). Erosion cuts into the **cones** of **volcanoes**. It also takes away soft rocks faster than hard rocks, so that hard **volcanic** rocks stand out in the landscape (*see:* **Igneous rock**). **Dikes** and **sills**, as well as volcanic **plugs**, are all striking landscape features that developed from the effects of erosion carrying away the soft rocks around them.

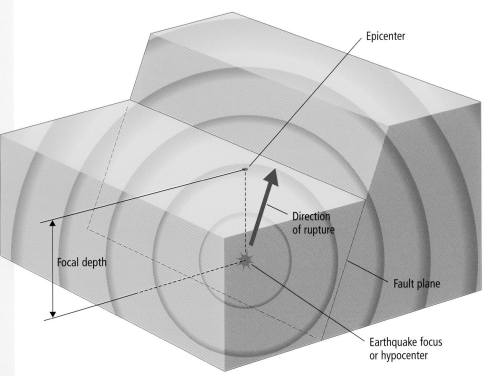

Epicenter

Direction of rupture

Focal depth

Fault plane

Earthquake focus or hypocenter

Eruption

An eruption occurs when a **volcano** expels solid or liquid materials. The liquid may be in the form of **lava** that flows from the volcano, or it may be in the form of fine **ash** thrown high into the air with **gases** to make tall clouds.

An eruption normally begins with a short amount of warning in the form of **earthquakes**. The earthquakes signal that pressure is building inside the **magma chamber** deep below the volcano, and that the pressure is starting to cause the **rocks to fracture**. Each earthquake is a place where rocks are cracking apart.

Once the pressure inside the magma chamber is great enough, the **magma** forces its way to the surface. Volcanoes may have a number of "false starts"; but when the main eruption begins, it is often with sudden and spectacular force.

The kind of eruption that occurs depends on the material making up the magma. There are several types of eruption shown here.

The eruption continues as long as the pressure in the magma chamber is high enough, but gradually the pressure is reduced, and the eruption slows down and finally stops.

Most eruptions last for between a day or two to a month or two.

Mount St. Helens is a good example of this process. The volcano had been thought **dormant** before the eruption of 1980. The first warning signs that something was going to happen occurred when ice started to melt off the summit, and a small **crater** developed. Steam started to come from the small crater.

Earthquakes then started to happen close to the volcano, showing that the pressure of magma was

causing the rocks in the volcano to crack. Then a bulge developed on one side, where the weakest rocks were located. Finally, the rocks of the bulge were weakened so much they fell away, allowing the eruption to begin out of the side of the **cone**, producing a **pyroclastic flow**.

The eruption then continued directly upward, sending **gases** and **ash** high into the sky. After some weeks a small amount of lava was seen in the new crater. Then, over the following months the volcano stopped sending up ash and steam, and the eruption stopped.

(*For other erupted material see:* **Bomb**; **Glowing avalanche**; **Lahar**; **Lapilli**; **Pele's hair**; **Pele's tears**; **Pumice**; **Pyroclastic material**; **Scoria**; **Spatter**; **Tephra**.)

(*For eruption types see:* **Explosive**; **Hawaiian-type**; **Icelandic-type**; **Pelean-type**; **Phreatic**; **Plinian-type**; **Strombolian-type**; **Vulcanian-type**.)

▼ **Eruption**—The main types of eruption.

Plinian-type volcanic eruption

Pelean-type volcanic eruption

Shield-type volcanic eruption

▲ **Eruption**—A spatter cone near the top of the summit complex of Hawaii. Eruptions like this contribute to the gently sloping cones typical of Hawaiian-type volcanoes.

◀ **Eruption**—The initial phase of the Mount St. Helens eruption was a Pelean-type, but later the eruption changed and became a Plinian-type. The result of the Pelean-type eruption was to blast part of the cone away.

Eruption cloud

The cloud of **gases** and **ash** created by the **explosive eruption** of a **volcano**.

Explosive eruption

A violent **eruption** of sticky (**acid**) **lava** that involves the sudden ejection of huge volumes of **ash** and **gas**. Very little **lava** flows at the start of an explosive eruption.

There are two reasons for an explosive eruption. First, the more acid and full of gas the **magma** is, the harder it is for it to flow quickly out of the **vent** of the **volcano** before the gases in it expand. Second, the old **plug** that is sealing the **vent** may be difficult to dislodge, so that more pressure has to build up in the **magma chamber** below in order to break through the plug.

It may help to imagine an explosive volcano as a soft-drink bottle. The magma chamber is the bottle, the volcano is the neck of the bottle, and the cap is the plug blocking the vent. If you shake the bottle vigorously and then undo the cap quickly, a large amount of liquid comes out, propelled in part by the gas in the liquid. To begin with, the froth explodes out in all directions, and only later on does it flow down the side of the bottle.

There are three types of explosive eruption:

1. When gas and ash are thrown out of the vent in the form of a dark, swirling cloud over the volcano. This is the least violent type (*see:* **Vulcanian-** and **Strombolian-type**).
2. When clouds explode sideways because the vent remains blocked. Gases, ash, and **rock** behave like a fast-moving liquid that rolls down the side of the volcano, rather like a **glowing avalanche** (*see:* **Pelean-type**).
3. When gases shoot up into the air in a giant column (*see:* **Plinian-type**).

▼ **Explosive eruption**—An explosive eruption occurs when gas-rich magma reaches the surface.

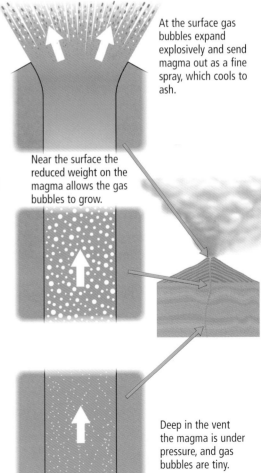

At the surface gas bubbles expand explosively and send magma out as a fine spray, which cools to ash.

Near the surface the reduced weight on the magma allows the gas bubbles to grow.

Deep in the vent the magma is under pressure, and gas bubbles are tiny.

Extinct volcano

A **volcano** that has shown no signs of activity in historic times (*see:* **Volcanic activity**). (*Compare with:* **Dormant volcano**.)

Extrusive rock

An **igneous rock** that has solidified on the surface of the Earth. **Lava** is the extrusive rock that flows from an **eruption**. (*See also:* **Intrusive rock**.)

F

Fault

A deep **fracture** or zone of fractures in **rock** where one **plate** has moved relative to another (*see:* **Fracture zone**). It represents a weak place in the **crust**.

There are several different types of fault. Transcurrent faults, also known as strike-slip faults and transverse faults, are vertical fractures where the slabs have mostly moved horizontally, like pushing two books next to one another on a table. Dip-slip faults are sloping fractures where the slabs have mostly moved vertically. If the uppermost block moves down, it produces a **normal fault**, while if the top slides up, it produces a **reversed fault**. Whenever the fault moves, it produces **earthquakes**.

(*See also:* **Active fault; Blind fault; Creep; Fault scarp; Fault zone; Locked fault; Thrust fault**.)

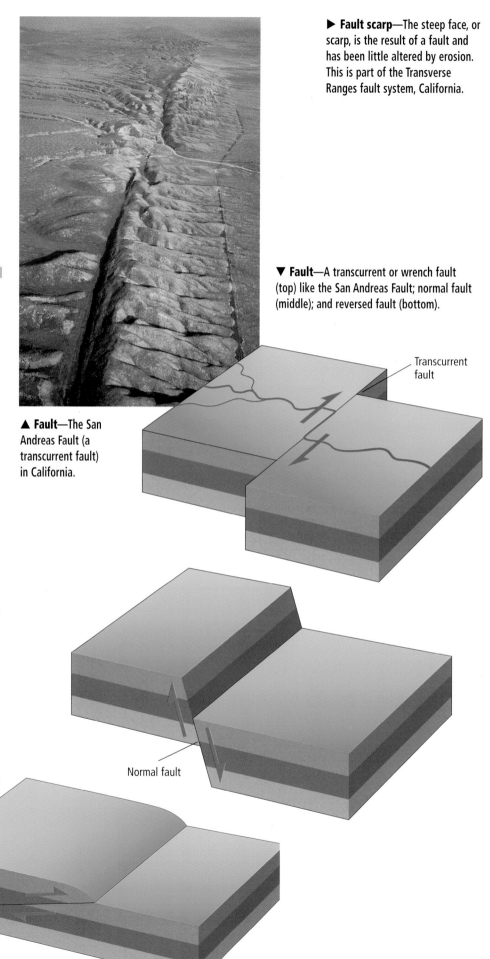

► Fault scarp—The steep face, or scarp, is the result of a fault and has been little altered by erosion. This is part of the Transverse Ranges fault system, California.

▼ Fault—A transcurrent or wrench fault (top) like the San Andreas Fault; normal fault (middle); and reversed fault (bottom).

▲ Fault—The San Andreas Fault (a transcurrent fault) in California.

Transcurrent fault

Normal fault

Reversed fault

Fault scarp

Fault scarp

A long, straight, steep slope in the landscape that has been produced by a **fault**.

Fault zone

A region in which there are many **faults**. Faults in a fault zone often run parallel to one another, but they may also cross. Not all faults in a fault zone need be the same age. One of the most well-known faults, the **San Andreas Fault** in California, is actually a fault zone.

Feldspars

The most common **minerals** found in the Earth's **crust**. About half of all the Earth's crustal **rocks** are made from feldspars (named after the German for "field crystals"). There are two kinds. One kind (orthoclase feldspar) is white or gray, and the other kind (plagioclase feldspar) is usually pink. You cannot see into a feldspar—it is opaque. But the surface shines (it has a luster like porcelain), and it breaks up into flat-faced blocks.

Feldspars are reasonably hard. They are, however, easily weathered and are the "weak link"

in many otherwise resistant rocks, breaking down into clay minerals and allowing the rest of the rock to fall apart.

Ferromagnesian minerals

A group of **minerals** containing a large proportion of iron and magnesium.

Examples include **augite**, **hornblende**, and **olivine**. In general, they are very difficult to tell apart because they are all green, dark-green, or black and often occur only as small crystals. Nevertheless, they form a major part of many **igneous rocks** and affect the overall color of the **rock**. For example, **basalt** appears black because it contains predominantly ferromagnesian minerals.

First motion

The direction of ground motion of the first part of the **P wave** as it arrives at the **seismograph**. If it is upward, then the **earthquake** has occurred because the ground has pulled apart. If the first motion is downward, the earthquake has resulted from the ground being compressed.

Fissure

A substantial crack in a **rock**; and also a long crack or opening on a **volcano**. **Lava fountains** and **lava flows** commonly pour out of fissures during **fissure eruptions**. If the fissure remains underground, **magma** may flow into it and create a **dike**. (*See also:* **Hot spot** and **Spreading boundary**.)

Fissure eruption

An **eruption** that occurs when **lava** flows from a long crack, or **fissure**, in the Earth's **crust** rather than from a single chimneylike **vent**. (*See also:* **Oceanic spreading ridge**.)

The material that comes from a fissure eruption is always very runny **basalt lava**. (*See also:* **Dike** and **Dike swarm**.)

A fissure occurs because the crust is splitting apart, and most fissures therefore occur at **spreading boundaries** between tectonic **plates**. The most spectacular example of this occurs in Iceland.

Fissure eruptions do not build up **volcanic cones** because the lava is far too runny. Instead, the lava spurts up out of the fissure in a series of **lava fountains** of orange and yellow-hot rock (**incandescent**) and then floods over the landscape, burying everything in its path. (*See also:* **Hawaiian-type** and **Icelandic-type eruption**.)

The floods of lava from fissure eruptions that have built up the whole of Iceland are small compared to the floods of lava from fissures in the more distant past.

The majority of fissure eruptions happen under the sea. Fissure eruptions are responsible for making all of the floor of the world's oceans. However, they are not often observed or studied because the eruptions occur quietly under thousands of meters of water.

Fissure eruptions occasionally occur on land, as is shown in Iceland. In the past they have been so huge that they have covered hundreds of thousands of square kilometers. The world's largest example is the Deccan Traps in India, where **lava flows** have built up **rock** thousands of meters thick. This is the result of a **flood basalt** eruption and is a form of **supervolcano**. There are other gigantic lava plateaus. In North America basalt occupies much of the basins of the Columbia and Snake Rivers. In the United Kingdom Fingal's Cave and the Giant's Causeway are both parts of old fissure eruptions.

Fortunately, these giant eruptions are rare, and none has happened on land in recorded history. If it did, the loss of life might be immense, while the heat released might alter the climate.

▼ **Fissure eruption**—Fissure eruptions are spectacular flows of lava from long fissures. The basaltic lava that flows from them can travel long distances very quickly.

▼ **Fissure eruption**—The nature of a fissure eruption.

▶ **Fissure eruption**—The result of a fissure eruption allowing basalts to flood over the landscape, Columbia Plateau, Idaho.

Flood basalt

An **eruption** of **basalt** that occurs very occasionally, when a large **fissure** opens in the Earth's **crust**. Vast volumes of extremely runny **lava** flood over the landscape, often extending to cover millions of square kilometers (*see:* **Supervolcano**). The largest of them makes up much of the Deccan region of India, but large flood basalts also occur in the Columbia-Snake River basin of the northwestern United States. (*See also:* **Fissure eruption**.)

Focal depth

The depth of an **earthquake focus** below the surface. (*See also:* **Epicenter**.)

Focus

The origin of an **earthquake**, directly below the **epicenter**. Another word for **hypocenter**. (*See also:* **Focal depth** and **Shadow zone**.)

Foreshocks

Relatively smaller **earthquakes** that occur before the **main shock**. Not all main shocks have foreshocks, and so foreshocks can only sometimes be used to give warning of a major event.

Fracture

A substantial break across a **rock**. Rock that is fractured is broken extensively by Earth movements; and although the rock itself may be hard, the fractures represent lines of weakness that may make it easier for the rock to be eroded. (*See also:* **Fault** and **Fracture zone**.)

Fracture zone

A region of **rock** in which **fractures** are common. Fracture zones are particularly common in folded rock and near **faults**. Fracture zones are places where rocks have been broken and are more liable to **erosion**. They are often connected with bands of low land. River valleys sometimes follow fracture zones. (*See also:* **Oceanic spreading ridge**.)

Fumarole

A small opening or **vent** from which hot **gases** puff their way to the surface. Fumaroles may occur in places where there are active **volcanoes**, or they may occur where there is no **volcanic activity**. However, even if there is no active volcano present, they represent gases reaching the surface from a **magma chamber** far below. Fumaroles are often found in areas where there are **geysers** and **mud pools**. Examples, include Bumpass Hell in Lassen National Park, California, and Yellowstone National Park, Wyoming.

▼ **Fumarole**—Fumaroles are mainly steam with sulfur gases.

G

Gabbro

An **alkaline igneous rock**, typically showing dark-colored **crystals**; it is made of the same **minerals** as **basalt**, but has large crystals because it solidified slowly deep underground (*see:* **Augite** and **Hornblende**).

Although gabbro makes up a thick layer below the basalt that covers the ocean floor, it is rare to find gabbro on land. Outcrops of gabbro mainly occur where parts of ancient ocean **plates** have buckled upward and become mountains.

Gas

One of the three states of matter; the other two are liquid and solid. In the case of **volcanic activity** gases are connected to places where **magma** is close to the surface. In these places liquids find their way to the surface, often as volcanic **eruptions**. These liquids have substances in them that are only liquid under great pressure. When these substances reach the surface and are not under so much pressure, they change into gases. Sulfur dioxide and hydrogen sulfide are two of the gases found in eruptions and also in **fumaroles**. Hydrogen sulfide smells of rotten eggs, while sulfur dioxide is a brown gas. Many other gases are also released, but they are colorless and have no smell. Carbon dioxide and oxygen are two such gases. (*See also:* **Glowing avalanche**.)

▶ **Geyser**—Old Faithful Geyser, Yellowstone National Park.

Geyser

Hot springs that send powerful jets of steam and water into the air from time to time. They are found in places where hot **volcanic rocks** are quite close to the surface. Many geysers are found in the same areas as **volcanoes**, or where volcanoes were once active below the surface and where **magma chambers** still contain hot rocks.

Geysers are not the only signs that there are hot rocks near the surface. Hot springs and **mud pools** are in fact much more common than geysers. Sometimes, when there is little water available, puffs of steam, or **gases** with breathtaking sulfurous smells, are the only signs. They are called **fumaroles**.

Magma chambers are also places where great chemical changes occur. As steam, gases, and water move through the rock, they dissolve many of the **minerals** from the rock, so the geysers are far from being pure water. Rather, they contain a wealth of dissolved minerals.

As the hot, mineral-laden water comes to the surface, it cools.

Because cool water can hold less dissolved material than hot water, the minerals are deposited on the land around the geyser. The minerals build up into geyser cones.

Yellowstone National Park in Wyoming is one of the most famous areas of hot springs and geysers in the world. The magma that heats the water lies below the park. The volcano that was fed by the magma last had a major **eruption** 600,000 years ago, but minor eruptions have occurred since.

The rocks below the surface remain hot; and when cool water from the surface seeps down to them, they heat it up and cause geysers.

The geysers at Yellowstone lie inside a **caldera** 45km by 75km in size. The geysers now rise from the floor of the caldera. Old Faithful, the most famous of the geysers, gushes upward, around 35m to 50m high, every 40 to 80 minutes, although most geysers are not as regular as this.

Water and steam

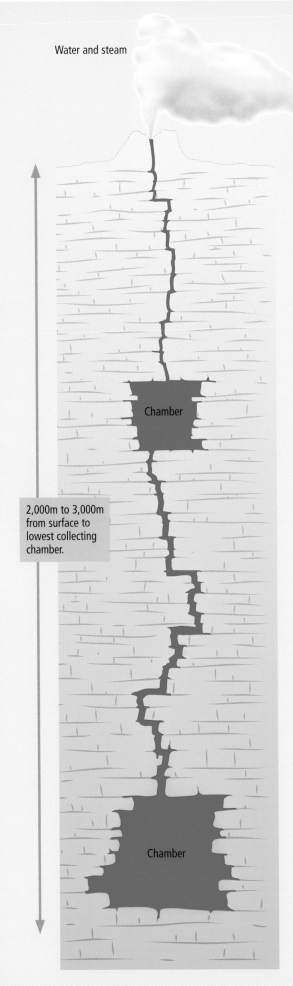

2,000m to 3,000m from surface to lowest collecting chamber.

Chamber

Chamber

7—Some of the minerals in the water are deposited around the geyser to build up the cone.

6—The steam and water shoot out of the geyser until there is no steam left.

5—Eventually, the pressure gets so high the water begins to boil. This causes cold water to be thrown out as a fountain, along with the hot water that has turned to steam.

4—The weight of cold water seeping into the upper passageway from above acts like a lid on a pressure cooker. The water below gets hotter and hotter, but it cannot escape.

3—Heated passageways continue to heat the trapped water.

2—Water heats up to above boiling point in a chamber created where rock has been dissolved away.

1—Water seeps through the rocks and builds up in underground passageways.

▲ **Geyser**—The seven stages of geyser activity.

▲ **Geyser**—Castle Geyser, Yellowstone National Park.

Glass, volcanic

Lava that has solidified very quickly and has not had time to develop separate **crystals** properly. **Obsidian** is a volcanic glass.

▲ **Glass, volcanic**—Obsidian is a natural glass. It is opaque because the glass contains a huge number of natural flaws.

Glowing avalanche

A mixture of hot **gas** and **rock** that travels at great speed down the side of a **volcano**, just like an avalanche. It is also known as a **pyroclastic flow**. It is one of the most destructive results of an **eruption**.

Volcanoes sometimes explode sideways, sending gas, **ash**, and other forms of **tephra** hurtling down the side of the volcano instead of up into the air. This fiery mixture moves with great speed and behaves like a snow avalanche, but moving even faster and with even greater destructive power. It reaches temperatures approaching 1,000°C.

The **explosive eruptions** that cause glowing avalanches occur when acid **magma** that is full of gases builds up enough pressure to blow the top of the volcano apart. The pressure that builds up before this happens can be enormous and can cause any weak rock above the **magma chamber** to **fracture**. This is why just before explosive eruptions there are often many small **earthquakes**. Each earthquake marks the snapping of rocks close to the volcano or in the **cone**.

When a route to the surface is found, the volcano erupts like a shaken soft-drink bottle when the cap is taken off.

Sometimes the rocks in the side of the volcano are weaker than the **plug** of **lava** sealing the main **vent**. When this is the case, the new magma can burst through the side of the volcanic cone, and the full force of the eruption is sent out sideways, rather than upward. It is like firing an enormous gun at the surrounding landscape.

First, a chunk of the cone is blown away. Then the gases, ash, and rock are mixed together and thrown sideways with tremendous force. Everything standing above the ground—trees, houses, and so on—is blown away, and the land is left bare for tens of kilometers from the volcano.

One of the most devastating eruptions in historic times that included a glowing avalanche happened in 1902 on the Caribbean island of Martinique. The volcano

▼ **Glowing avalanche** —The formation of a glowing avalanche.

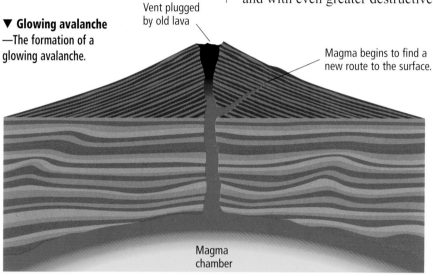

Vent plugged by old lava

Magma begins to find a new route to the surface.

Magma chamber

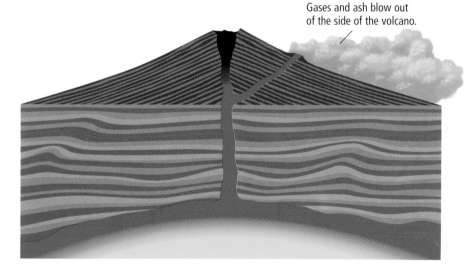

Gases and ash blow out of the side of the volcano.

◀ **Glowing avalanche**—The Mount Pelée eruption on Martinique. This picture shows the devastation in the immediate aftermath.

on this island is called Mont Pelée, and it rises some 1,400m. On May 8, 1902, after many warning signs that a major eruption was about to happen, the volcano suddenly exploded, not from the top, but out of the side of the cone. A cloud of scalding gases and ash raced down the mountainside and engulfed the port town of Saint-Pierre. Within a few seconds 30,000 people had been killed, about a sixth of the population of the island. The only person left alive was a prisoner who was being kept in a dungeon. The dungeon protected him from the full force of the blast.

The name of the mountain is now used to describe a violent

▶ **Granite**—Granite is the most widespread igneous rock on land. It is easily distinguished by its interlocking pink or grey (feldspar), black (biotite), and glassy (quartz) crystals.

eruption that includes a glowing avalanche—**Pelean-type**.

In 1980 Mount St. Helens, Washington, erupted with a similar glowing avalanche, but in this case the destruction was confined to a forest wilderness. Nevertheless, over 30 million trees were demolished within seconds.

Granite

An **acidic**, **igneous rock** formed deep below the surface of the Earth, mainly in the **magma chambers** that once fed **volcanoes**. Because this material was insulated from the surface, it cooled slowly, giving time for **crystals** to form.

The biggest crystals in a granite are usually **feldspar**. They make the opaque gray, white, or pink shapes in a granite. Black **micas** form much smaller crystals (*see:* **Biotite**). A mass of crystalline **quartz** (looking like grayish glass) fills in the spaces between the feldspar and mica crystals. (*See also:* **Phenocryst**.)

Granites are easily recognized and colorful **rocks**. Large masses of granite are found in **batholiths**.

Ground failure

A general term for any kind of landslide, **liquefaction**, or other effect that occurs due to the shaking of an **earthquake**.

H

Hawaiian-type eruption

A name for a **volcanic eruption** that mainly consists of **lava fountains**. (*See also:* **Hot spot**.)

▶ **Hawaiian-type eruption**— Eruptions of lava in the form of lines of lava fountains are among the most characteristic features of a Hawaiian-type eruption.

Hornblende

A dark-green **silicate mineral** containing sodium, potassium, calcium, magnesium, iron, and aluminum. Hornblende is a common mineral in **rocks** like **basalt** and **gabbro**.

Hot spot

A place where a fixed **mantle magma** fountain, or plume, reaches the surface. One of the best examples is the Hawaiian Islands.

Hydrothermal

A change brought about in a **rock** or **mineral** due to the action of superheated mineral-rich fluids, usually water.

When molten rock forces its way to the surface, it makes up the sticky material that will later become a **volcanic eruption** and is also a part of other liquid mixtures that can easily force their way into small cracks in the neighboring rocks. They are called hydrothermal (hot water) liquids. They contain rich concentrations of metals. When they later cool and solidify in the surrounding rocks, they form rich mineral deposits that can be mined for metals such as gold, silver, copper, zinc, and lead.

Hypocenter

Another word for the **focus** of an **earthquake**. It is the point within the Earth where an earthquake **rupture** starts. (*See also:* **Epicenter**.)

I

Icelandic-type eruption

A name given to a type of **fissure eruption** common in Iceland.

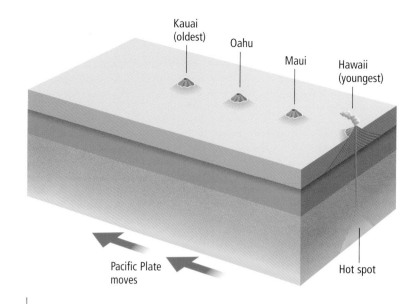

▲ **Hot spot**—The hot spot below the Pacific Ocean has produced the Hawaiian chain of volcanoes. There is probably another hotspot under the Pacific Northwest, still marked by Yellowstone National Park.

▼ **Igneous rock**—The diagram shows the main forms of intrusive and extrusive rocks in their position of formation.

Igneous rock

Rock formed when **magma** cools and solidifies. The word igneous means fire-baked. All igneous rocks either began in **magma chambers** or **volcanoes**.

There is a wide variety of igneous rocks. The most common are **basalt** and **granite**. Basalt is the most common form of **lava** that flows from volcanoes. Granite is the cold remains of extinct magma chambers.

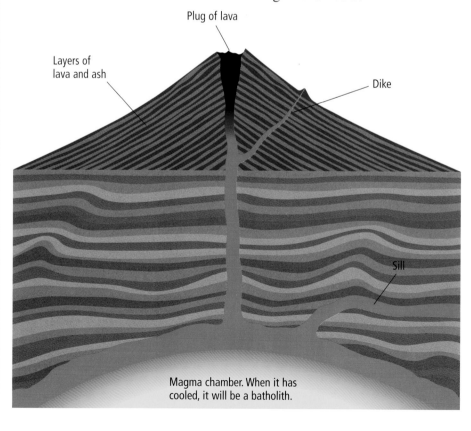

Igneous rocks include **extrusive volcanic** rocks such as lava and **ash** and **intrusive rocks** formed underground such as **dikes**, **sills**, and **batholiths**.

(*For other types of igneous rock see:* **Acid**; **Alkaline**; **Basic**; **Diorite**; **Gabbro**; **Pegmatite**; **Plutonic**.)

Rock from volcanoes

Volcanic rocks—lava and ash—are made of **crystals** so tiny they can often only be seen with a microscope. That is because lava and ash cool very quickly in the air, and there is no time for big crystals to form.

One of the most common features of volcanic rocks are small

Diorite

cavities. They are bubbles of **gas** that were trapped inside the rock as it cooled (*see:* **Amygdule** and **Vesicle**).

The most common volcanic rock is a black lava called basalt. Most of the world's ocean floors are covered in basalt that has erupted from undersea volcanoes. In some places **flood basalt** has formed huge sheets of rocks thousands of square kilometers in area and hundreds of meters thick. It is common in places like Hawaii, Iceland, and India. It flows from supervolcanoes during "supereruptions."

Rock of dikes and sills

Some magma pushes into gaps between rocks but never reaches the surface. The sheets of magma formed this way are called dikes and sills.

This magma cools in the ground, and so there is more time for crystals to form. The rocks are still dark colored, but have bigger crystals in them.

Rock of magma chambers

When a magma chamber becomes extinct, it may take millions of years for the chamber to cool. There is plenty of time for large crystals to form. The most common of these rocks is called granite. It is usually pink and gray, and contains glassy **minerals**.

Incandescent

Glowing red, orange, yellow, or white as a result of high temperature. Incandescent lava can be seen during a **fissure eruption**, **glowing avalanche**, and **pyroclastic flow**.

Intensity

A number (written as a Roman numeral) that refers to the severity of an **earthquake** (*see:* **Modified Mercalli scale**).

(*See also:* **Isoseismal**.)

Intrusive rock, intrusion

Igneous rocks that have formed from cooling **magma** that has forced its way through other **rocks**.

The main types of intrusion are **batholiths**, **bosses**, **laccoliths**, **sills**, and **dikes**. Batholiths are the largest intrusions. They are bodies of **granite** that were formerly **magma chambers** supplying volcanoes. As magma forced its way from these chambers into weak areas in the surrounding rock, it created many other kinds of intrusion. Sheets of igneous rock formed by prying the surrounding rocks apart are called **sills** and **laccoliths**; those that cut across the surrounding rocks and form wall-like sheets are called **dikes**.

Gabbro

Andesite

▲ **Igneous rock**—Igneous rocks all have interlocking crystals. The main differences between them involve the size of the crystals and the proportion of dark- to light-colored minerals. Dark color and large crystals typify gabbro (middle), an igneous rock that forms underground in the oceans. Rocks of dikes and sills often have medium-sized or small crystals because they cooled quickly; this is diorite (top). Rocks formed from lava that flowed on the surface have bubbles (vesicles) and tiny crystals. This is andesite (bottom).

► **Island arc**—Where ocean and continental plates collide, volcanoes form in long arcs. The Aleutian Islands form one such arc.

Kamchatka Peninsula

Aleutian Islands

Alaska

Island arc

A crescent pattern of **volcanic** islands. Island arcs occur where an ocean **plate** is pushing below a continental plate. The best examples surround the Pacific Ocean (*see:* **Pacific Ring of Fire**).

(*See also:* **Arc**; **Ocean trench**; **Subduction zone**.)

Isoseismal

A line on a map showing places of equal **earthquake intensity**. They can be thought of as "contours" of earthquake intensity.

L

Laccolith

A lens-shaped body of **intrusive igneous rock** with a dome-shaped upper surface and a flat bottom surface. It is a relatively uncommon feature.

Lahar

A flow of **volcanic igneous rock** fragments and water down the sides of a **volcano**. It can cause great destruction. Lahars are caused by melting ice on top of volcanic mountains mixing with loose debris on the sides. **Eruptions** will often melt an ice cap quickly, releasing huge amounts of water.

Lapilli

Rock fragments between 2mm and 64mm in diameter that are ejected from a **volcano** during an **explosive eruption**. Lapilli means "little stones" in Italian. It is a form of **tephra**.

Lava

Molten rock that reaches the Earth's surface. It can be runny or sticky depending on the **minerals** it contains.

Lava is the liquid part of the material called **magma** that comes from deep within the Earth. It normally flows from a volcano at temperatures of about 1,000°C.

There are many kinds of lava, but it is easiest to think of lava as belonging to two main groups: **Acid lava** and **basic lava**. Both types cool to form **extrusive rock**.

Acid lava is sticky and **viscous**. It flows from **central vent volcanoes** in the form of slowly moving **tongues**. Acid lava moves only a few meters a day. It only adds small amounts of material to the **cones** of volcanoes. Much of

the sticky lava in volcanoes cools to a brown rock called **andesite**, named for the Andes Mountains, where it is common.

Basic lava, which is runny, flows quickly from gently sloping volcanoes or **fissures** and often appears as rivers or sheets.

Basic lava can reach speeds of many kilometers an hour. The most common form of basic lava is **basalt**. It is also by far the most common form of lava in the world. Basalt makes huge sheets of rock both on the ocean floor and on land.

Basalt lava sheets can have a smooth surface, in which case it is called **pahoehoe lava**. Alternatively,

▼ **Lava**—As lava emerges from a volcano, it is so hot that its color is yellow or red. As it flows away from the vent, it cools, solidifies and turns black.

▼ **Lava**—As this fast flowing river of runny lava quickly changes course, it engulfs nearby forests that have grown on old lava flows. This is Hawaii.

it can have a broken surface, in which case it is called **aa lava**.

There are also some special, and very interesting, forms of lava. If lava cools very quickly, it forms a black volcanic **glass** with no crystals or air bubbles in it. It is called **obsidian**. The surface of sticky lava is often puffed up by **gases** expanding in the molten lava. When it cools, it produces a very lightweight material called **pumice**.

Here are two examples of places with different types of lava: Hawaii is the largest of the Hawaiian chain of volcanic islands in the Pacific Ocean. The magma that rises to the surface there produces runny, basalt lava. The runniness of the lava can be seen in several ways. First, the lava spurts up above the **vent** as a **lava fountain**. Then it runs in rivers down the sides of the volcanoes for many tens of kilometers. (*See also:* **Shield volcano**.)

Mount Pinatubo, in the Philippines, is a major volcano

in eastern Asia. The magma from Mount Pinatubo is sticky, and most of it is ejected as tiny fragments of lava that cool to produce **ash**. The lava that flows from the vent toward the end of the **eruption** rarely travels far.

(*For other types of lava see:* **Ash**; **Bomb**; **Lava flow**; **Lava lake**; **Lava tube**; **Pele's hair**; **Pele's tears**; **Pillow lava**; **Rhyolite**; **Spatter**.)

▼ **Lava**—The Hawaiian Islands' lava flows boil the water as they ooze into the sea. The solidifying lava adds new land.

Lava flow

A stream of **lava** from an active **volcano**. It can take the form of a **tongue**, a river, or a sheet of lava. (*See also:* **Eruption**.)

Lava fountain

A jet of molten **lava** produced during an **eruption** of **basic lava**. (*See also:* **Fissure**; **Fissure eruption**; **Hawaiian-type eruption**.)

Lava lake

A pool of **lava** that builds up in some **craters** during an **eruption** of runny **basic** lava.

Lava tube

An underground tunnel formed when the surface of **lava** cooled and solidified while the rest of the lava continued to flow.

▼ **Lava flow**—This lava flow on Hawaii has formed a sheet. The shiny surface of the new lava is glinting in the Sun, making it look white.

▼ **Lava tube**—A thin crust is all that is between these scientists and a river of molten lava flowing inside a lava tube.

Liquefaction

The loss of strength of a soil or **rock** due to ground shaking during an **earthquake**. Liquefaction turns material into a kind of quicksand, allowing buildings to sink into their foundations.

Lithosphere

That part of the **crust** and upper **mantle** which is brittle and makes up the tectonic **plates**. The lithosphere is about 100km thick.

Locked fault

A **fault** that is not slipping because the sides of the fault are locked by the friction between them. When locked faults do move, they often produce very large **earthquakes**. Parts of the **San Andreas Fault** in California appear to be locked.

Love wave, L wave

A major type of surface **earthquake** wave that shakes the ground surface at right angles to the direction in which the wave is traveling. It is named after A.E.H. Love (1863-1940), the English mathematician who discovered it. (*See also:* **Body wave; P wave; Rayleigh wave; Seismic waves; Seismograph; Surface wave; S wave**.)

◄ **Lava tube**—Lava tubes can be tens of meters in diameter.

M

Magma

Any mixture of liquid, **gases**, and chunks of solid **rock** beneath the Earth's surface. Magma is the source of all of the Earth's **igneous rocks**. It **erupts** onto the Earth's surface as **lava**, pushes into **fractures** in underground rocks as **sills** and **dikes** and solidifies underground to form **batholiths**.

Many volcanoes are fed by vast underground caverns filled with magma. They are called **magma chambers**. A magma chamber may be hundreds of kilometers long and feed many **volcanoes**.

The kind of rock that forms from magma depends on the composition of the magma and on how it cools. The composition depends, in turn, on the materials from which the magma is made. Magmas are partly molten material from the **mantle** and partly rock from the **crust**. Some magmas—called acid magmas—contain a large proportion of **silica**; they are acid and very sticky. They are magmas that produce **explosive eruptions**. By contrast, some magmas—called basic magmas—contain little crustal material, are very runny, and produce hardly any explosions at all.

Hot, watery liquids called **hydrothermal** fluids may also rise from the magma and flow into **fissures** in the crust. When they cool and become solid, they provide rich deposits of metals. They are called **mineral** veins.

Magma chamber

A large cavity melted in the Earth's **crust** that is filled with **magma**. Many magma chambers formed in the shape of plumes of magma that have melted and risen from the **mantle** to the upper part of the crust. When magma stops rising into the chamber, any **volcanoes** it is supplying become **extinct**, and the magma remaining in the chamber solidifies to form a **granite batholith**.

Magnitude

A number that describes the strength of an **earthquake**. Magnitude is based on the maximum motion recorded by a **seismograph**. The most commonly used scale is the **Richter scale**.

Main shock

The largest **earthquake** that occurs during a ground **rupture**. Smaller **foreshocks** may go before it, and **aftershocks** may follow it. The main shock is the one used to find the magnitude on the **Richter scale**.

Mantle

The layer of the Earth between the **crust** and the **core**. It is approximately 2,900km thick and is the largest of the Earth's major layers by volume. The mantle is divided into a number of zones. The part of the mantle just below the crust is of most importance in causing **volcanoes** and **earthquakes** (see: **Asthenosphere** and **Lithosphere**). Here, parts of the mantle are molten, and most of it can move very slowly. This region moves with a churning motion called convection. In convection the hot material rises, while the cooler material sinks. The heat for convection is produced deep within the Earth. The

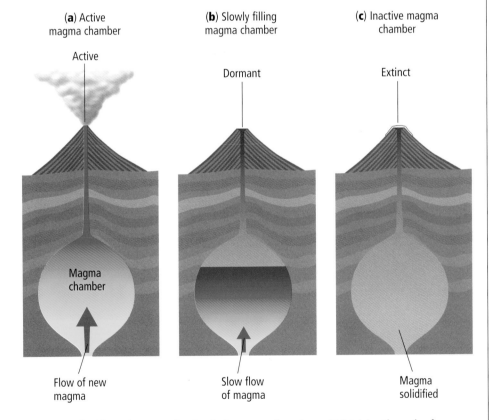

(**a**) Active magma chamber

Active

Magma chamber

Flow of new magma

(**b**) Slowly filling magma chamber

Dormant

Slow flow of magma

(**c**) Inactive magma chamber

Extinct

Magma solidified

▲ **Magma chamber**—A magma chamber is the soruce of a volcano. Maintaining the cycle of a volcanic eruption depends on what happens inside the magma chamber. (**a**) If the magma chamber fills and increases pressure on the plug blocking the vent of the volcano until the volcano erupts, that produces an active volcano. (**b**) The magma chamber begins to refill. If the refilling happens slowly, the volcano appears dormant. (**c**) The volcano ceases to erupt because no new magma reaches the chamber.

movement can be compared to the way that water churns over when heated in a saucepan. Where hot rock rises, plumes of molten rock cause the crust to bulge up. They are the **spreading boundaries** that occur, for the most part, in the center of the oceans and create long lines of **volcanic** mountains often called **midocean ridges**, such as the Mid-Atlantic Ridge. Smaller plumes of molten rock rise under the continents and form more isolated volcanoes.

(*See also:* **Mohorovicic discontinuity** and **Plate**.)

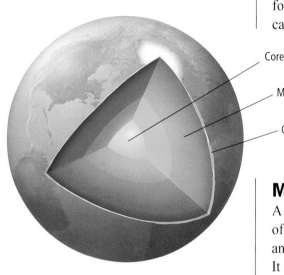

▲ **Mantle**—The mantle makes up the largest part of the Earth. The upper mantle is probably molten at least in places. It is the material that experiences convection currents and is responsible for the movement of the Earth's crustal plates.

Mica

Any sheetlike **mineral** that breaks up into flakes. There are many micas, but the most common are brown, white, or colorless **muscovite** and black **biotite**. Micas are soft, but quite resistant to weathering. They are flat, platelike **crystals** that normally form small, shiny specks in a **rock**. They are very common in **igneous rocks**, for example, **granite**.

Midocean ridge

A long mountain chain on the ocean floor where **basalt** periodically erupts, forming new oceanic **crust**. These ridges are connected to plumes of **magma** rising from the **mantle**. The largest of these is the Mid-Atlantic Ridge. It is the longest mountain system in the world.

Mineral

From a geologist's point of view a mineral is any naturally occurring nonliving substance of definite chemical composition—for example, calcite (calcium carbonate).

Core

Mantle

Crust

Modified Mercalli scale

A scale for measuring the impact of an **earthquake** on people and places (*see:* Table right). It is composed of 12 levels of increasing **intensity** ranging from imperceptible, designated by Roman numeral I, to catastrophic destruction, designated by XII. It is not a scientific scale because it is based on how severe the earthquake effects are on a place, and that might be influenced by such things as how well the buildings are constructed. It is used in part because, until the last century, when the **seismograph** was developed, there was no scientific way of comparing earthquakes, and people had to rely only on descriptions of the effects. The Mercalli scale allows rough comparisons between the earthquakes in the past and those of modern times.

Modified Mercalli Intensity scale

I.   People do not feel any Earth movement.

II. A few people might notice movement if they are at rest or on the upper floors of tall buildings.

III. Many people indoors feel movement. Hanging objects swing back and forth. People outdoors might not realize that an earthquake is occurring.

IV. Most people indoors feel movement. Hanging objects swing. Dishes, windows, and doors rattle. The earthquake feels like a heavy truck hitting the walls. A few people outdoors may feel movement. Parked cars rock.

V.   Almost everyone feels movement. Sleeping people are awakened. Doors swing open or close. Dishes are broken. Pictures on the wall move. Small objects move or are turned over. Trees might shake. Liquids might spill out of open containers.

VI. Everyone feels movement. People have trouble walking. Objects fall from shelves. Pictures fall off the walls. Furniture moves. Plaster in walls might crack. Trees and bushes shake. Damage is slight in poorly built buildings. No structural damage.

VII. People have difficulty standing. Drivers feel their cars shaking. Some furniture breaks. Loose bricks fall from buildings. Damage is slight to moderate in well-built buildings; considerable in poorly built buildings.

VIII. Drivers have trouble steering. Houses that are not bolted down might shift on their foundations. Tall structures such as towers and chimneys might twist and fall. Well-built buildings suffer slight damage. Poorly built structures suffer severe damage. Tree branches break. Hillsides might crack if the ground is wet. Water levels in wells might change.

IX. Well-built buildings suffer considerable damage. Houses that are not bolted down move off their foundations. Some underground pipes are broken. The ground cracks. Reservoirs suffer serious damage.

X.   Most buildings and their foundations are destroyed. Some bridges are destroyed. Dams are seriously damaged. Large landslides occur. Water is thrown on the banks of canals, rivers, and lakes. The ground cracks in large areas. Railroad tracks are bent slightly.

XI. Most buildings collapse. Some bridges are destroyed. Large cracks appear in the ground. Underground pipelines are destroyed. Railroad tracks are badly bent.

XII. Almost everything is destroyed. Objects are thrown into the air. The ground moves in waves or ripples. Large amounts of rock may move.

The Mercalli scale does not use any instrumental measurements. Thus seismologists can use newspaper accounts, diaries, and other historical records to make intensity ratings of past earthquakes. This is helpful for estimating future hazards.

Mohorovicic discontinuity, Moho

The boundary surface (between 25km and 60km deep beneath the continents and between 5km and 8km deep beneath the ocean floor) that separates the Earth's **crust** from the underlying **mantle**. Named after Andrija Mohorovicic (1857-1936), a Croatian seismologist. It is often just referred to as the Moho. At this depth the properties of the **rocks** change markedly, in part because the rocks are less brittle and able to move without **fracturing**.

Mud pool

A pool of heated water and mud that forms above some hot rock areas. Rainwater and melting snow fill the **vent** of a **fumarole**. As sulfur gases dissolve in the water, they make it very acid. The acid water weathers the surrounding **rock**, breaking the rock down, and creating mud. The mud acts like a lid, sealing in the rising **gases**. The mud spurts up and splatters when the pressure of the trapped gases becomes sufficient to push their way up through the mud.

Mud pools, unlike **geysers** and hot springs, change their character throughout the year depending on how much rainfall or snowmelt there has been.

Muscovite

A brown form of **mica**. It is a common **mineral** in **igneous rocks**. The name muscovite comes from Muscovy glass, because it was once used instead of glass in Russia.

N

Normal fault

A **fault** in which one part of the Earth's **crust** has slipped down the face of another. It is the most common kind of fault and results from parts of the crust pulling apart. (*Compare to:* **Reversed fault**.) (*See also:* **Rift, rift valley**.)

O

Obsidian

A natural **volcanic glass** (**rock**). Glassy rocks are often associated with rapid cooling of very sticky **acid lava** containing water. This **lava** contains about 10% water, which keeps it mobile. When the **magma** reaches the surface, the water boils off. As a result, the magma increases rapidly in stickiness and, at the same time, cools. These are the conditions that produce volcanic glass. You cannot see through the glass because it contains too many tiny **crystals**. As a result, there is no clear path for light to pass through.

Oceanic spreading ridge

A **fracture zone** that occurs within the oceans and marks the place where two **plates** are pulling apart. It occurs where **magma** flows up from the **mantle** and is a common source of **fissure eruptions**. The Mid-Atlantic Ridge is the biggest example of a spreading ridge.

◄▲ **Mud pool**—Mud pools at Bumpass Hell, California.

Ocean trench

A deep, steep-sided trough in the ocean floor formed where a slab, or **plate**, containing oceanic **crust** pushes beneath another plate. Most ocean trenches are found parallel to, and just offshore of, strings of islands (**island arcs**). These trenches are the deepest places in the oceans. (*See also:* **Subduction zone**.)

Olivine

A group of magnesium iron **silicate minerals** that have an olive color. They mostly form small **crystals** in dark-colored **igneous rocks** such as **basalt**.

P

Pacific Ring of Fire

The ring of **volcanoes** and **volcanic activity** that circles the Pacific Ocean (*see:* **Island arc**). The pattern is created by the collision of the Pacific Ocean **plate** with its neighboring plates.

Volcanoes along the Ring of Fire are found throughout the Andes Mountains, in western North America, on the islands off the coast of Asia, such as Japan and the Philippines, and across Indonesia and Papua New Guinea to New Zealand.

Because so many of the volcanoes are active, and therefore send out plumes of fiery **lava**, the ring of volcanoes is often called the Pacific Ring of Fire.

The pattern of volcanoes provides many clues about the way that the Earth works. Because volcanoes only **erupt** where there is a line of weakness in the **crust**, the pattern of volcanoes identifies major lines of weakness in the crust. The pattern around the Pacific Ocean provides evidence that one of the Earth's great plates lies under the Pacific Ocean. The Ring of Fire is also a place of intense **earthquake** activity—90% of the world's earthquakes occur on the Ring of Fire.

Pahoehoe lava

A form of **basalt lava** that flows in thin sheets and has a smooth surface. Compare with **aa lava**.

▲▼ **Pahoehoe lava**—This form of basaltic lava forms a smooth surface.

Lava moves fairly quickly.

A thin crust forms on the surface.

▼ **Pacific Ring of Fire**—The Ring of Fire includes both island arcs and continental mountain ranges, active volcanoes, and frequent earthquakes. On this map the pattern of the Ring of Fire is marked by earthquakes.

Parasitic cone

A side **cone** on a **volcano**.

Pegmatite

An **igneous rock** (for example, a **dike**) of extremely coarse **crystals**.

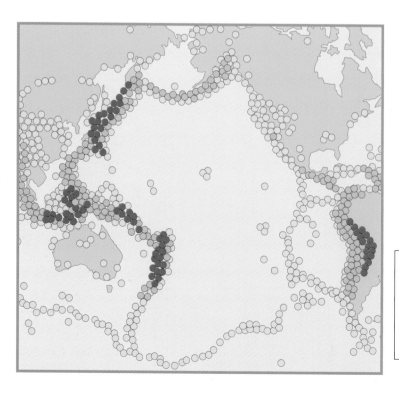

Depth of earthquake

○ 0–69km

◉ 70–299km

● 300–800km

Pelean-type eruption

A violent **explosive eruption** dominated by **pyroclastic flows**. (*See also:* **Glowing avalanche**.) Mount St. Helens erupted in this way in 1980.

▲ Pele's hair

Pele's hair

Thin strands of **lava** that cool as they fly through the air during an **eruption** of lava. (*See also:* **Tephra**.)

Pele's tears

Small pieces of **lava** that are thrown clear of **lava fountains** and cool as they fly through the air to make teardrop-shaped **bombs**. (*See also:* **Tephra**.)

Phenocryst

An especially large **crystal** embedded in smaller **mineral** grains or in **igneous rock**. Phenocrysts are common in **granite**.

Phreatic eruption

Steam-driven explosions that occur when water beneath the ground is heated by **magma**. **Basalt** can superheat water to 1,170°C in this way, producing an explosive outburst of steam, water, **ash**, blocks, and **bombs**.

Pillow lava

Pillow-shaped masses of **lava** that form under water.

▲ **Phreatic eruption**—The Mount St. Helens eruption during a Phreatic (Plinian) eruption phase.

Pipe

(*See:* **Vent**.)

Plate

A large segment of the Earth's **crust** separated from other segments by deep **fractures** that extend from the surface to the **mantle** (*see:* **Lithosphere**). These segments are also called tectonic plates and crustal plates. The boundaries of plates are common locations for **volcanoes** and **earthquakes**.

The Earth's crust is quite thin, compared to the size of the planet, and it is made of brittle **rocks**. Movements in the molten material in the **mantle** below the crust are therefore able to split up the crust into the giant segments called plates (*see:* **Asthenosphere**).

On average, plates are dragged a few centimeters each year. This may not sound like much, but over millions of years it results in the movement of plates over large distances. The Atlantic Ocean, for example, has formed by this slow movement over the past 100 million years.

As the plates move, they pull apart in places. These areas are

◄ **Plate**—The surface crust is a thin layer that "floats" on the mantle below. Here the edges of the continental plates have been exaggerated to make them easier to see. Volcanoes occur at most edges of the crustal plates.

called **spreading boundaries**, and they allow **magma** to flow easily from the mantle to the surface. The lava flowing from **fissures** at spreading boundaries is always **basalt**.

Most spreading boundaries are under the oceans, where the crust is thin. **Eruptions** under the oceans are rarely noticed and only become obvious where the boundary is on land, as is the case in Iceland. As the plates pull apart, lava flows up the fissures to "seal the wound." This is why the ocean floor is made of **basalt** rock. Large earthquakes do not occur at spreading boundaries.

Where plates collide, one plate is usually pushed below another. At the same time, rocks that have formed on the seabed may be pushed up to form mountain ranges.

▼ **Plate**—The map shows the main plates and plate boundaries.

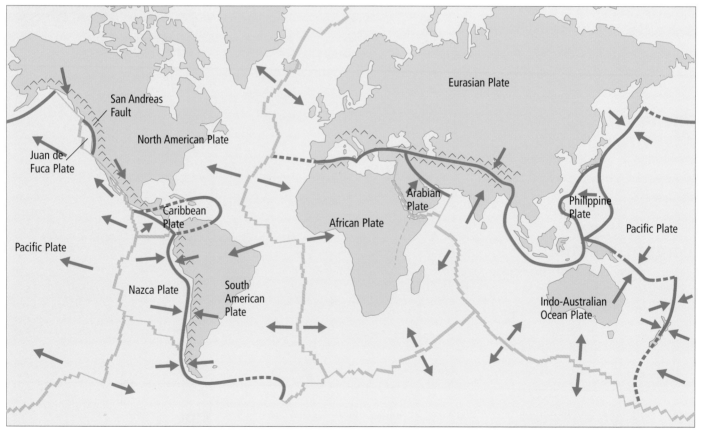

San Andreas Fault

North American Plate

Juan de Fuca Plate

Caribbean Plate

Pacific Plate

Nazca Plate

South American Plate

Eurasian Plate

Arabian Plate

African Plate

Philippine Plate

Pacific Plate

Indo-Australian Ocean Plate

〰〰〰 Constructive plate margins (oceanic ridges offset by transitional faults)

━━━ Destructive plate margins (oceanic trenches or continental collision zones)

∧∧∧∧ Fold mountain range

➝ Direction of plate movement

Examples of this include India, which is pushing against Asia to form the Himalayan Mountains, and Africa, which is pushing against Europe to form the Alps. Earthquakes and volcanoes are common in such places, but volcanoes are made of sticky, **acid magma** and are more explosive and violent than volcanoes at spreading boundaries.

In some places plates do not spread apart or collide, but simply scrape past one another. This is happening along the coast of California. This does not create volcanoes, but instead causes many earthquakes. The earthquakes in California mainly occur along the **San Andreas Fault**.

(*See also:* **Benioff zone**; **Colliding boundary**; **Creep**; **Destructive plate boundary**; **Oceanic spreading ridge**; **Ocean trench**; **Pacific Ring of Fire**; **Plate tectonics**; **Rift, rift valley**; **Rifting**; **Seismic zone**; **Subduction**; **Subduction zone**.)

Plate tectonics

The theory that the Earth's **crust** and upper **mantle** (the **lithosphere**) are broken into a number of more or less rigid, but constantly moving, slabs or **plates**.

Plinian-type eruption

An **explosive eruption** that typically sends a column of **ash** high into the air. The ash may reach as high as 30km above the **volcano**.

Plug

The solidified core of an **extinct volcano**. Sometimes the phrase volcanic neck is used instead of volcanic plug.

All volcanoes erupt through the pipes, or **vents**, that connect them to the surface. Toward the end of the **eruption** the **magma chamber** that supplies the liquid rock loses pressure and is no longer able to push liquid rock out of the vent. As a result, the magma and any broken remains of the vent walls that were torn free during the eruption stay in the vent, slowly cooling until they become solid **rock**.

A **volcanic cone** is mainly composed of layers of **ash** and **lava**. Ash, in particular, is easily worn away. By contrast, the material that plugs the vent of the volcano is often very tough and better able to stand up to the action of rivers and the weather (**erosion**). The plug of material is therefore often the last part of a volcano to remain.

Volcanic plugs can make striking pillars of rock in the landscape. Some of them have flat tops. Some plugs have been used as fortresses and others as places for religious buildings such as churches.

The most famous church sited on a plug is at Le Puy in the Massif Central Mountains of France. The best-preserved plug is probably Ship Rock, New Mexico.

▼ **Plug**—Ship Rock, New Mexico, is a plug with radiating dikes.

▼ **Plug**—A volcanic plug at Le Puy, France. A fortification used this high point to command the area in the Middle Ages.

Dike

Ship Rock plug

Dike

Plutonic rock

An **igneous rock** that has solidified at great depth and contains large **crystals** due to the slowness of cooling. The name comes from Pluto, the Roman god of the underworld.

Intrusive rocks may cool relatively quickly if they are simply thin sheets of **magma** squeezed between layers of cold **rock**. This happens when **dikes** and **sills** are formed. **Diorite** is an example of this kind of rock. Large masses of magma—for example, the **magma chambers** that are the sources of **volcanoes**—cool very slowly at the end of their active lives, and that gives time for crystals to grow larger. **Granite** is an example of this kind of plutonic rock.

Pumice

Any **volcanic** material that contains so many **gas** bubbles that it can float on water. Some pumice is thrown out by volcanic **eruption**; some is formed on the surface of **lava flows**.

P wave, primary wave, primary seismic wave

A **body wave** produced during an **earthquake**. P waves travel through the ground from the source of the earthquake and shake the surface to and fro in the same direction as the wave is moving (*see:* **First motion**).

P waves are the fastest body waves. They can travel through all layers of the Earth and are generally felt at the surface as a thump before the main earthquake. They give a few seconds notice of the arrival of larger **surface waves**. (*See also:* **Seismic waves** and **S wave**.)

Pyroclastic

A general term used to describe anything that is thrown out of a **volcano** during an **explosive eruption**; *pyro* means "fire" and *clast* means "broken piece."

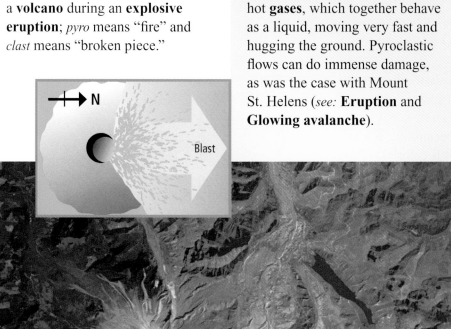

Pyroclastic flow

Solid material ejected from a **volcano**, combined with searingly hot **gases**, which together behave as a liquid, moving very fast and hugging the ground. Pyroclastic flows can do immense damage, as was the case with Mount St. Helens (*see:* **Eruption** and **Glowing avalanche**).

▲▼▶ **Pyroclastic flow**—These pictures show the 1980 pyroclastic flow during the eruption of Mount St. Helens, Washington State. The blast zone was to the right (north), as shown in the inset diagram. Notice that the area to the left of the cone is undisturbed, while a great piece has been blown out of the right-hand side of the cone (a new plug of lava has formed in the center of the cone). A large area of forest was flattened and covered in pyroclastic material.

Pyroclastic material

Any solid material ejected from a **volcano**.

Q

Quartz

The **mineral** silicon dioxide. Quartz is easy to recognize because it has a glassy appearance. It is colorless when pure, but impurities can give it a variety of colors, especially brown. Quartz almost always forms irregular grains, rather than **crystals**, with well-defined faces. That is because quartz has a relatively low melting point and is the last mineral to crystallize in an **igneous rock**. It fills all the remaining gaps between the crystals that have already formed. Quartz is quite hard, and its compact structure makes it extremely resistant to **erosion**.

▶ **Refraction**—Seismic waves travel through the crust and are changed in speed and direction (refracted) by the materials of the Earth. While earthquake waves travel right through to the other side of the Earth, some regions fall into "shadow zones" and never record an earthquake at all.

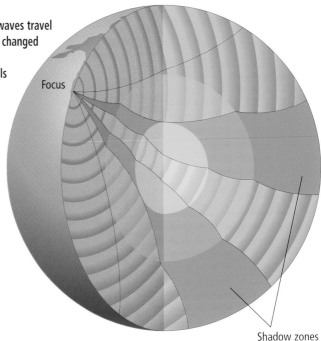

Focus

Shadow zones

R

Rayleigh wave

A type of **surface wave** produced by an **earthquake**. Named after Lord Rayleigh (1842-1919), the English physicist who predicted its existence.

Rayleigh waves move forward with an oval motion similar to the waves caused when a stone is dropped into a pond. They are the slowest, but often the largest and most destructive, of earthquake waves. Rayleigh waves are usually felt as a rolling or rocking motion. During major earthquakes they can even be seen as they approach by the way the ground humps up as each wave crest passes. (*See also:* **Seismic waves**.)

Reflection

The rebounding of a wave. In the case of **earthquakes seismic waves** are reflected from different kinds of **rock** inside the Earth. By studying the pattern of reflected waves, scientists can better understand the composition of the inside of the Earth.

Refraction

The bending of **seismic waves** as they move between materials with different properties. In particular, the pattern of refracted waves leaves a **shadow zone** on the side of the Earth opposite the source of the **earthquake**. This has helped locate the boundaries between **crust**, **mantle**, and **core**.

Reversed fault

A **fault** in which one slab of the Earth's **crust** rides up over another. Reversed faults are only common during **plate** collision. (*See also:* **Normal fault**.)

Rhyolite

An **acid lava** whose **mineral** content is similar to **granite**. It is a very sticky **lava** (*see:* **Viscous, viscosity**) associated with **explosive eruptions**. It does not form extensive flows and quickly solidifies, often before extensive crystals can form. It has a number of glassy variants that form on the surface, including **obsidian** and **pumice**.

Richter scale

The system used to measure the energy in an **earthquake** (*see:* Table right). Developed by Charles Richter, an American, in 1935. (*See also:* **Magnitude** and **Modified Mercalli scale**.)

Rift, rift valley

A large trench in the **crust** usually caused by tension. Rift valleys are common where the **crust** is spreading. Parallel **normal faults** allow some blocks to sink between others and form valleys. Volcanoes often form as **magma** rises up along fault lines. The East African Rift Valley is the world's largest continental rift valley. (*See also:* **Rifting**.)

Rifting

The process of crustal stretching that causes blocks of **crust** to sink, creating **rift valleys**.

Ring of Fire

(*See:* **Pacific Ring of Fire**.)

Rock

The solid material on the Earth's surface. Rocks are classified into **igneous** (formed from **magma**), metamorphic (formed by great heat and pressure), and sedimentary (formed as layers laid down mostly on ocean floors). (*See also:* **Erosion**.)

The Richter scale

This is a scale for measuring the intensity of an earthquake. It was developed by American scientist Dr. Charles F. Richter. It is a measure of the energy released by an earthquake.

The Richter scale is not an even scale. Each unit on it is ten times bigger than the one below it. This allows a huge range of values to be placed on one scale.

Earthquake magnitudes are not very closely connected to the effect of the earthquake. The effect depends on the kind of rock in which the earthquake occurred.

Magnitudes	Effects
Less than 3.5	Generally not felt, but recorded.
3.5–5.4	Often felt, but rarely causes damage.
5.5–6.0	Can cause major damage to poorly constructed buildings; has little effect on well-constructed buildings.
6.1–6.9	Can be destructive in areas up to about 50 kilometers from the focus.
7.0–7.9	Major earthquake. Can cause serious damage over larger areas.
8+	Great earthquake. Can cause serious damage in areas more than 100 kilometers from the focus.

The table below describes the energy in an earthquake in terms of an equivalent amount of TNT explosive (after USGS).

Richter scale	TNT for seismic magnitude	Example Energy yield (approximate)
-1.5	18 grams	Breaking a rock on a lab table
1.0	15 kilograms	Large blast at a construction site
1.5	150 kilograms	
2.0	1 ton	Large quarry or mine blast
2.5	4.6 tons	
3.0	29 tons	
3.5	73 tons	
4.0	1,000 tons	Small nuclear weapon
4.5	5,100 tons	Average tornado (total energy)
5.0	32,000 tons	
5.5	80,000 tons	Little Skull Mtn., NV, Quake, 1992
6.0	1 million tons	Double Spring Flat, NV, Quake, 1994
6.5	5 million tons	Northridge, CA, Quake, 1994
7.0	32 million tons	Hyogo-Ken Nanbu, Japan, Quake, 1995; Largest thermonuclear weapon
7.5	160 million tons	Landers, CA, Quake, 1992
8.0	1 billion tons	San Francisco, CA, Quake, 1906
8.5	5 billion tons	Anchorage, AK, Quake, 1964
9.0	32 billion tons	Chilean Quake, 1960
10.0	1 trillion tons	(San Andreas type fault circling Earth)
12.0	160 trillion tons	(Sunlight received by the Earth every day)

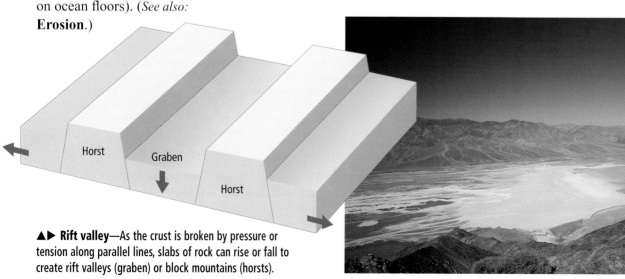

▲▶ **Rift valley**—As the crust is broken by pressure or tension along parallel lines, slabs of rock can rise or fall to create rift valleys (graben) or block mountains (horsts).

Horst

Graben

Horst

Rupture

The area where **rocks** move over each other during an **earthquake**. (*See also:* **Epicenter** and **Hypocenter**.)

S

San Andreas Fault

The name of one of the world's most famous **fault zones**. It runs close to the coast in California. The San Andreas Fault system is more that 1,300km long and up to 16km deep.

The average rate of motion across the San Andreas Fault during the past 3 million years has been 56mm/yr (about the same rate as fingernails grow). This rate means that in 15 million years Los Angeles will have moved north and will lie in the Pacific Ocean, opposite San Francisco.

Scoria

A general term for all the coarse, rough, often foamlike **rock** material associated with an **eruption**. It may be in the form of **bombs** thrown out of a **volcano** or may be carried on the surface of **lava** during an eruption. (*See also:* **Tephra**.)

▲ **Seamount**—Seamounts are volcanic islands that rise from the ocean bed. The volcanoes may or may not be active. Many seamounts are ringed by coral reefs. Many do not reach the surface at all.

Seamount

A **volcano** that rises from the seabed. Many Pacific islands are the tops of seamounts.

Seiche

The to-and-fro movement of an enclosed body of water as a result of the water being affected by **earthquake** waves. Lakes and estuaries are all prone to this effect. The swimming pool at the University of Arizona in Tucson lost water from a seiche caused by the 1985 Mexico earthquake—2,000km away.

Seismic deformation

Earthquake waves cause **rocks** to change shape, or deform, in two ways: short-term change as the waves pass through an area, and long-term change due to the movement of the **fault** on which the earthquake took place.

The long-term change can sometimes be spotted as a break in railroad tracks or the shifting of the course of a river.

▼▶ **Scoria**—Fragments of foamy lava.

Seismic gap

A part of an **active fault** where there have been no **earthquakes** in recent times. A seismic gap is a place where the fault is probably **locked** temporarily. When and if it should become active again, large earthquakes are the likely result.

Seismic waves

A technical term for the waves produced by an **earthquake**. There are two kinds of seismic waves: **surface waves** and **body waves**. All of the waves travel through the ground at different speeds and reach the surface at different times after the earthquake occurred. The compressional **P waves** travel fastest, at somewhere between 1.5 and 8km/sec. Shear **S waves** move at about two-thirds the speed of P waves. The main waves that cause damage are **surface waves** (**Rayleigh waves** and **Love waves**). They begin as body waves, but change character as they reach the surface.

The difference in speed between waves accounts for the way they are spaced out along a trace on a **seismogram**.

About 90% of the earthquake's energy is used in moving the **rocks** along a line of **rupture**. The remaining 10% is used in generating the **shock waves**.

(*See also:* **Amplification**; **Reflection**; **Refraction**; **Seiche**.)

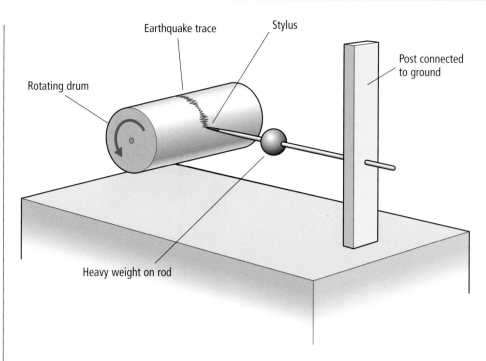

Earthquake trace · Stylus · Rotating drum · Post connected to ground · Heavy weight on rod

Seismic zone

A region where the cause of **earthquakes** is the same. For example, where they share a common **plate** boundary.

Seismogram

The trace, or series of wavy lines drawn on paper, produced by a **seismograph** during an **earthquake**. (*See also:* **Amplitude**.)

▼ Seismogram—P, S, and surface waves reach a seismograph at different times. P waves arrive first, then S waves, with surface waves being last. As the graph shows, the amplitude of the surface waves is far greater than the P or S waves, and they last far longer. That is why the surface waves are the most destructive part of an earthquake.

▲ Seismograph—A seismograph uses the principle of inertia to remain still while the earth is shaking.

Seismograph

An instrument designed to record the **seismic waves** produced by an **earthquake**.

A seismograph works on the principle that it takes a long time to set a suspended weight in motion. This means that the weight can be thought of as stationary even while the ground around it is moving violently.

One of the best ways to use this principle is by means of a simple pendulum. When the ground shakes, the base and frame of the

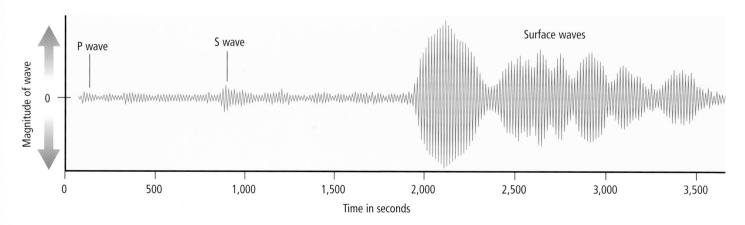

seismograph move with it, but the pendulum remains still until long after the earthquake is over. As the instrument frame moves around, the relative movement between frame and pendulum can be recorded on a paper drum or by electronic equipment. The record produced is called a **seismogram**. The first pendulum seismograph was built in 1751.

Each seismograph recording station has three seismographs, one detecting the north-south movement, another detecting east-west movement, and the third detecting up-and-down motions. From the traces it is possible to find the distance, direction, **Richter scale magnitude**, and type of **fault** of the earthquake.

By using a network of seismographs, it is possible to find the precise location of the origin of the earthquake.

(*See also:* **First motion**.)

Shadow zone

The region of the Earth that experiences no **shocks** after an **earthquake**. It lies directly opposite the **focus** of the earthquake on the far side of the Earth. (*See also:* **Refraction**.)

Shallow earthquakes

Earthquakes with a **focus** fewer than 70km below the surface. (*See also:* **Crust**.)

Shield volcano

A broad, gently sloping **volcano**, usually built up by many fluid **lava flows** of **basalt**. Mauna Loa, Hawaii, is an example of a shield volcano.

Shock wave

A common term for the effect of **earthquake** waves. (*See also:* **Seismic waves**.)

Silica, silicate

The **mineral** silicon dioxide. Silica is a very common mineral, occurring frequently as glassy **quartz** in **igneous rocks**. A silicate is any mineral that contains silica. (*See also:* **Acid lava/acid rock**; **Augite**; **Feldspar**; **Hornblende**; **Mica**; **Olivine**.)

Sill

A sheet of **intrusive igneous rock** (typically **diorite**) that has been injected between layers of rock.

The pressure in a **magma chamber** is fearsome and capable of causing the surrounding rock layers to crack apart. If the magma finds a weakness between two layers (beds) of rock, it may push the uppermost layer aside and inject molten material in between the two rock layers. The magma will then bake the rocks on either side, often making them very tough. Then the magma cools into a hard rock. This layer of rock is called a sill. Notice that when it is formed, a sill has a "roof" and a "floor."

Sill rocks, like **dike** rocks, are often tough and stand up to **erosion** better than other rocks. So, as the landscape eventually gets worn down, the sills and dikes become exposed and stand up in the landscape as natural "ridges."

You can tell a sill from a dike because a dike cuts across other rocks, while a sill pries rock layers apart and lies parallel to neighboring rock layers.

You cannot tell a dike from a sill simply by whether it makes a wall or a ledge. That is because the rocks may have been turned on their sides after they were formed.

Sills often occur in the same place as dikes, and they also make prominent ridges in the landscape. The most famous sill (called the Great Whin Sill) was followed by the Romans when they built Hadrian's wall across northern England some 2,000 years ago.

▼ **Sill**—Sills are sheets of igneous rocks that have forced their way in between the surrounding rocks. If they are tougher than the rocks on either side, they will stand out as a sloping ridge or even a ledge horizontal to a waterfall. The Great Whin Sill in England was used by Roman Emperor Hadrian as the foundation for his famous wall that divided England from Scotland.

Sill

▲ **Spatter**—The material that splashes from a vent.

Spatter

Splashes of liquid **lava** produced close to a **vent** during an **eruption**. They often make a spatter **cone**.

Spreading boundary

A line on which two **plates** are moving apart. **Basaltic magma** wells up in the **fissure** created by the parting plates. Most spreading boundaries are on ocean floors. They are the most common places for **fissure eruptions**. (*See also:* **Oceanic spreading ridge**; **Rift, rift valley**.)

Stock

A vertical protrusion of a **batholith** that reaches close to the surface. Similar to **boss**.

Stratovolcano

A steep-sided "classic" **volcano**, usually formed into a **cone** and made of both **lava** and **ash**. The same as **composite volcano** and **central vent volcano**.

Strombolian-type eruption

A type of **volcanic eruption** in which there are periodic bursts of fluid **lava**, usually **basalt**, from a **crater**. The volcanic eruption is **explosive** enough to send out volcanic **bombs**. The Italian volcano Stromboli, after which this eruption type is named, sends out fiery bombs and is known as "the lighthouse of the Mediterranean Sea."

Strong motion

Earthquake motion big enough to cause damage to buildings.

Subduction

The process of one tectonic **plate** descending beneath another.

Subduction zone

The part of the Earth's surface along which two tectonic **plates** collide, and one tectonic plate descends into the **mantle**. A **subduction** zone is often marked by a deep, narrow trench called an **ocean trench**. As one plate is pushed back into the mantle, **crust** melts and begins to rise to the surface, forming **volcanoes**. The volcanoes often form a pattern in the shape of an **arc**. Most **volcanoes** occur parallel to and inland from the boundary between the two colliding plates. Some subduction zones create wide areas

▶ **Subduction zone**—The place on the Earth's surface where one crustal plate is forced below another. Subduction zones are places where mountains form, earthquakes are common, and explosive volcanoes occur. They are geologically the world's most spectacularly active places. The Pacific Ring of Fire is the most active of all.

of sinking land that fill with sediment. When these trenches are finally crushed together, they form the bulk of a new mountain range.

Supervolcano

A **volcano** that produces an **eruption** on quite a different scale from the eruptions we normally experience. There are two kinds of supervolcanoes. One kind occurs when a large **fissure** opens up suddenly at a spreading **plate** boundary, providing immediate access from the **mantle** to the Earth's surface (*see:* **Fissure eruption**). As a result **basalt** literally floods out of the ground, covering hundreds of thousands of square kilometers, possibly in a matter of days or weeks (*see:* **Flood basalt**). The trap, or basalt plateau, landscapes are examples of this. The amount of heat released during this kind of event could change the Earth's climate.

The other kind of supereruption emerges from a **central vent volcano** that emits **ash** and **gases** far in excess of anything normally experienced. This kind of volcano can throw huge volumes of ash into the air and cover hundreds of thousands of square kilometers of land in ash, while at the same time sending fine ash into the air and reducing the amount of sunlight that reaches the Earth's surface. Such supervolcanoes may have been responsible for mass extinctions of life that have occurred from time to time during the Earth's history.

Both kinds of supervolcano are extremely rare, and none has occurred within recorded history. However, the geological record makes it clear that they have occurred every few millions of years and will presumably happen in the future.

Surface wave

Any one of a number of **seismic waves**, such as **Love waves** or **Rayleigh waves**, that shake the ground surface just after an **earthquake**.

S wave, shear or secondary seismic wave

This kind of **body wave** carries energy through the Earth like a rope being shaken. S waves cannot travel through the outer core of the Earth because they cannot pass through fluids. (*See also:* **P wave** and **Seismic waves**.)

T

Tectonic plate

(*See:* **Plate**.)

Tephra

A general term for all fragmented **volcanic** material (for example, **ash** and **bombs**). Also called **ejecta**. (*See also:* **Agglomerate**; **Lapilli**; **Pele's hair**; **Pele's tears**; **Scoria**.)

Thrust fault

Another name for **reversed fault**, where one block pushes up and across another, shortening the **crust**. All thrust faults have a shallow angle to the horizontal.

Tongue, lava

A slow-moving flow of **lava** that streams down the side of a **volcano**.

Tsunami

A very large wave produced by an underwater **earthquake** or exploding **volcanic** island.

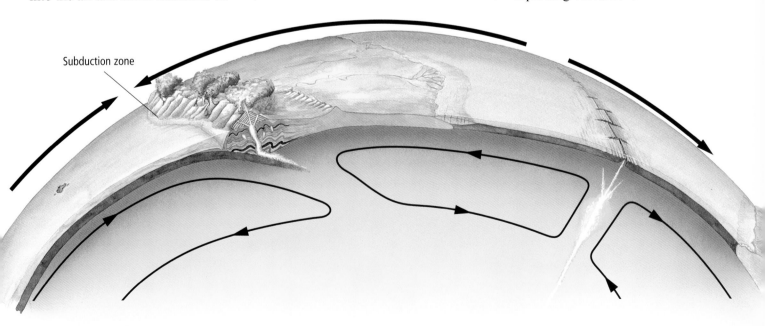

Subduction zone

Tuff

A **rock** made from **volcanic ash**. **Volcanic activity** produces a large amount of ash that settles over the landscape. It is particularly thick close to the **vent** of a **volcano**. After an **eruption** has ended, the ash begins to consolidate, and a later covering with **lava** or more ash will turn the first ash layer into a soft rock called tuff. This rock could be thought of as a sediment because it is deposited, but the material is entirely igneous, and it forms only at the time of an eruption.

V

Vent

An opening in the ground through which **magma** erupts or **volcanic gases** are emitted.

When an **eruption** takes place through a pipelike **vent**, the force of the explosion may tear the **rock** in the walls of the vent and widen it (*see:* **Crater**). The widening vent is a reason eruptions tend to get more powerful as they go on.

(*See also:* **Fumarole**.)

Vesicle

A bubble in a **volcanic rock** originally created by air trapped in the molten **lava**. (*See also:* **Amygdule** and **Basalt**.)

Viscous, viscosity

A term describing the thickness or stickiness of a liquid. It is applied to **lava** that is acidic and moves slowly. **Rhyolite** and **andesite** are viscous lavas. **Basalt**, which is a runny lava, is said to have a low viscosity.

Volcanic

Anything from, or of, a **volcano**. Volcanic **rocks** are **extrusive igneous rocks** (for example, **basalt**, **andesite**, and **rhyolite**) that cool as they are released at the Earth's surface—including those formed underwater. They typically have small crystals due to rapid cooling.

Volcanic activity

Volcanoes are often put in categories based on how active they appear to be. There are three categories: active, **dormant**, and **extinct**.

▼ **Volcanic activity**—Popocatepetl in Mexico during a phase of low activity.

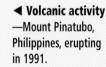

◄ **Volcanic activity** —Mount Pinatubo, Philippines, erupting in 1991.

Active
- Steam or ash visible.
- Eruption recorded in last 15 years.
- Frequent earthquakes.
- Lava flows common.
- Deposits of recent **lava** and **ash**.
- Smoke may be coming from the **vent**.
- There may be **earthquakes** focused below it.

Dormant
- Vent blocked.
- No eruption in last 15 years.
- Evidence of eruption in historical time.
- May erupt if magma can blow out the plug of rock in the vent.

Extinct
- Crater collapsed or vanished.
- No evidence of eruption in historical time.

All volcanoes have a "life cycle." They may be active for many thousands of years, but eventually the source of lava and ash gives out, and they first become dormant and then extinct.

In dormant volcanoes there is often a long pause between **eruptions**, since it can take a long time for the **magma chamber** to refill and come back to pressure. As a result, volcanoes may only erupt after several hundred years. This is why it is extremely difficult to tell the difference between a volcano that is active, dormant, or extinct. Many dormant volcanoes have snow and even glaciers on their summits.

In general, the longer the period between eruptions, the more violent the next eruption will be. As a result, nobody wants to make a mistake and declare a dormant volcano extinct when it might erupt

◄ **Volcanic activity**—Agathla Peak, Arizona, is an example of an extinct volcano. The cone has been stripped away by the weather, and all that remains is the plug that was once the vent of the volcano.

in a few days and threaten the lives of many people.

A good example of an extinct volcano is Arthur's Seat in Edinburgh, Scotland. All that is left are parts of the old **cone** and the **vent**.

A good example of a dormant volcano is Mount Ranier in the Cascade Mountains, Washington.

A good example of an active volcano is Mount St. Helens in the northwestern United States. When scientists surveyed the material of the cone before 1980, they felt that the volcano probably erupted once every hundred years or so. It had last erupted in the middle of the 19th century. Thus, although it was certainly inactive, the volcano was also certainly not extinct, and therefore must be dormant. In May 1980, with only a short period of warning, Mount St. Helens erupted in a spectacular way, devastating a wide area nearby with its **glowing avalanche** eruption.

Volcano

The name for a **cone** or other shape of mountain formed by **volcanic eruptions**.

The word volcano comes from the Italian mountain Vulcano. In ancient times this mountain was thought to be the entrance to the underworld, which was looked after by Vulcan, the blacksmith god.

If you were asked to draw a picture of a volcano, you would probably draw one with sides that get steeper toward the top (the cone) and then draw a depression (**crater**) in the top. This type of volcano is the most common land volcano. Such volcanoes are called **central vent volcanoes**, meaning that the **vent** that allows the **magma** to reach the surface comes

▼ **Volcano**—This satellite picture was taken in false-color to bring out the size, shape, and location of Mount Vesuvius, Italy, one of the world's most famous volcanoes. It is in the center of the picture, appearing as an isolated circular mountain, well away from other mountain ranges.

from a single pipe (vent) in the center. It is also called a **composite volcano** because it contains both **lava** and **ash**, and a **stratovolcano**, because the cone contains layers, or strata, of lava and ash. The other main type of volcano erupts from long **fissures**. The lava from these **fissure eruptions** forms **basalt** and very broad cones. They are often called **shield volcanoes**.

Volcanic cones are not built in a single eruption, but are formed by hundreds of eruptions over many thousands of years. Each eruption produces ash or lava. Some of the ash falls back down on the cone, adding a little more to the cone, while each flow of lava runs down over the sides of the cone and solidifies in **tongues**, like wax running from a candle.

The way that a volcano erupts affects the shape of the volcano it produces. If the volcano always

produces runny lava, the volcanic cone will be broad and flat; but if the volcano usually explodes and produces ash and sticky lava, then a steep-sided cone will be formed.

A few volcanoes, like Mount Fuji in Japan, have a beautifully simple shape. Most volcanoes are not as elegant because, in their long histories, eruptions have blown away the tops of their cones, or eruptions have occurred out of their sides. These events make the cones less symmetrical.

The material that erupts at the surface comes from deep underground, in a chamber filled with liquid rock under pressure. It is called a **magma chamber**. The way the material comes to the surface depends on how runny the **magma** is and how much **gas** it contains. If the magma has little gas and is very runny, it will produce a fountain of runny lava and have little explosive violence. If, on the other hand, the magma is sticky and full of gases that cannot easily escape, then, as the magma reaches the surface, the gases will burst out of the liquid, throwing it out into the air and producing a towering cloud of ash, gas, and steam. (*See also:* **Volcanic activity**.)

(*For other types of volcano see:* **Arc**; **Complex**; **Dormant**; **Explosive eruption**; **Extinct**; **Island arc**; **Pacific Ring of Fire**; **Parasitic cone**; **Seamount**; **Supervolcano**.)

(*For information on the source of volcanoes see:* **Crust**; **Plate**; **Subduction zone**.)

Vulcanian-type eruption

A type of **explosive eruption** that results in large amounts of **ash** as well as **lava**.

▼ **Volcano**—Kilauea, Hawaii, is an active volcano, with the last major eruption occurring in 1984.

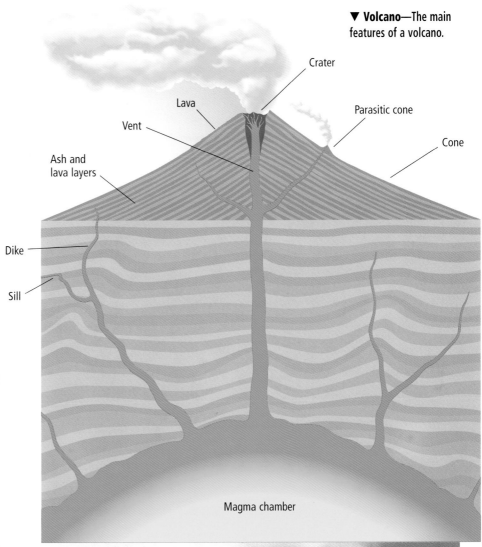

▼ **Volcano**—The main features of a volcano.

Crater

Lava

Vent

Parasitic cone

Cone

Ash and lava layers

Dike

Sill

Magma chamber

Index